PEOPLE
ARE YOUR
PROFIT

TRANSFORM YOUR
BIGGEST EXPENSE INTO
YOUR BIGGEST ASSET

MARK MITFORD, MA, MBA

People Are Your Profit

Copyright © 2026 by Mark Mitford

The Scripture quotation is from the Holy Bible, New International Version®, NIV® Copyright ©1973, 1978, 1984, 2011 by Biblica, Inc.® Used by permission. All rights reserved worldwide.

Published by
Illumify Media Global
www.IllumifyMedia.com
"Let's bring your book to life!"

Paperback ISBN: 978-1-970582-22-2

Cover design by Debbie Lewis

Printed in the United States of America

Contents

Foreword

In 2001, I bought a little software business that developed point of sale software for pizza restaurants. That business had thirteen employees, and the bookkeeper was acting as the de facto head of human resources, which didn't amount to much more than a payroll clerk.

In 2010, we started growing the company inorganically by acquisition. I had already done a massive rollup in the medical distribution industry and was anxious for another one. Within a relatively short period of time, we had acquired a handful of other businesses in and around the same space. One day, we had a particularly nasty HR problem with one of our California employees. That's when I realized that we had over 250 employees spread all across the US, and yet, our human resources "department" was still basically one payroll administrator. While that person was very good at her job, she didn't have the proper training to be an effective HR leader.

I had known Mark Mitford for many years. At the time, we were in a Bible study group together. One day, while Mark was between jobs, I asked him why he didn't hang his own shingle and work for small businesses like mine on a fractional basis. Small business owners have the same challenges as large businesses—only on a smaller scale. The thing we typically didn't have was executive level HR leadership because we couldn't support someone like Mark on a full-time basis.

A few months later, Mark showed up at my office and told me, "put your money where your mouth is." And, so, I became one of his earliest clients. His mission was simple: (1) point out my HR risks and blind spots and (2) train our internal HR person to be a true HR leader.

When I first engaged Mark as a fractional HR executive, my business was at a critical crossroads. Like many small to medium-sized (or middle market) businesses (SMBs), we were nimble but lacked the foundational HR processes necessary to scale effectively. Mark brought a Fortune 50 pedigree—honed at "best in class" companies like PepsiCo and Ericsson—and tailored it to the unique needs of a small growing firm. He taught us that culture is not an accident; it is an intentional, leadership-driven imperative that acts as a strategic differentiator from the competition. The principles Mark outlines in these chapters—moving from reactive whack-a-mole management to proactive people strategy—were instrumental in helping us build the high-performing team that eventually led to our successful exit in 2018.

This roadmap is more essential now than ever because the business environment has shifted drastically. With Gen Zers and millennials now comprising over half of the workforce, the old way of managing people simply no longer works. These employees are looking for more than a paycheck; they seek a strong sense of purpose, genuine work-life balance, and a culture that views them as people rather than just numbers.

In this book, Mark provides a timely guide for the modern leader to meet these needs while driving financial results. He breaks down complex concepts—from the Four Cs of onboarding to the strategic necessity of succession planning—into actionable building blocks.

There is a definite correlation between a great team and a growing, profitable business. If you get the people stuff right, a natural outcome will be more engaged employees and better leaders who know how to motivate those employees. And you don't get great people without having the right systems in place. It's only natural then that good HR systems and processes can lead to higher revenue and profits. If you want to stop simply filling seats and start building a resilient, sustainable legacy, the playbook is in your hands.

As for that payroll administrator, she's running HR for a division of the large, publicly traded business that acquired my company. I'm guessing that Mark's training and wisdom had more than a little something to do with that!

Tom Bronson, Serial Entrepreneur
Founder & CEO, Mastery Partners
Founder & CEO, Business Transitions Summit
Founding Partner, NorthStar Mergers & Acquisitions

Preface

My intent in writing this book is to give you a practical HR playbook on foundational processes and concepts within human resources (HR). After spending more than thirty-five years in my HR career, twenty of those working with SMB companies, over and over again I have seen that the department is the least structured in organizations of fewer than five hundred employees (SMBs) is the HR department. The irony is that most of a company's expenses are based on employee-related costs. Therefore, finding a way to optimize the efficiency of your employees just makes business sense. It's not extra fluff; it is a business imperative.

Creating an organization with highly skilled, engaged, employees working in the right roles and held accountable for their work makes all the difference. It sounds simple, but in reality, it is not. It's what every employer dreams of having but where most organizations fall woefully short. Where did things go so wrong? In many cases, they didn't *go* wrong. The HR systems and processes were never created to achieve these reasonable goals in the first place.

I began my HR career in 1990. Over the years, I have been truly blessed to work with several great organizations, such as PepsiCo, Ericsson, and Texas Instruments. I cut my teeth in HR working in larger Fortune 500 companies where I was privileged to be mentored, developed, and challenged by some of the leading HR minds industry-wide. The experience gained in my more than sixteen years with larger corporations was an unbelievable training ground to shape me into the HR leader and business owner I am today. I witnessed hyper growth to major restructuring and participated in two organizations that went through bankruptcy. That was very painful but nonetheless a formative learning experience.

Later, I pivoted to smaller companies that were lower- and middle-market sized (120-1,500 employees) where I held total HR responsibility. This was an exciting time in my career as I was able to have a major impact by creating and driving the people strategy in these businesses. In these smaller organizations, there was no HR strategy in place. It was only a transactional support function when I arrived.

In October 2013, I found myself looking for a new work opportunity, and God had a new and different plan for me. I had long thought of taking my high-level strategic HR experience and offering it to smaller businesses who lacked this expertise. With a stay-at-home wife and two college-bound daughters, the timing involved a leap of faith to start my own business. That was when HR Catalyst was born. My office was our kitchen table for several years.

I didn't know how to build a company, but I was highly motivated with God's help and the help of many friends! Honestly, things didn't start out quickly, but every prospect, referral, partner meeting, and networking event

I attended helped to shape HR Catalyst and our strategic value proposition.

Fast-forward, today our firm has worked with over 150 companies, helping them build and implement a people strategy for their business. I truly love working with business owners and helping solve their people challenges to become more successful. This brings me great joy.

The career path that God has taken me on is a combination of many human resource experiences over the last thirty-five years, which have come together to create the wisdom and insight that I am now sharing in this book. By investing in the people component of your business or organization, you can build resiliency, foster innovation, drive sustainable growth and increase your profitability. Thank you for joining me on this journey to discover how your employees can truly be the greatest asset in your organization.

"It is God who arms me with strength and
keeps my way secure."
— Psalm 18:32

Introduction

Over 34 million companies are considered small to medium-sized businesses or SMBs in the United States, which comprises 99.9 percent of all businesses in the US. They have under five hundred employees and in many cases offer a very basic human resource (HR) or employee infrastructure—payroll, healthcare benefits, hiring, and exiting or offboarding—to take care of their employees' needs.

Typically, HR is run by the chief financial officer (CFO), controller, or office manager, not a professionally trained HR person. The irony here is that the most expensive line item on any company's income statement is their people-related costs, typically comprising between 50 and 70 percent of their overall cost structure. CFOs, or controllers are great at understanding the financials of the company; they are not great at understanding the complexity of a company's culture, or how to select, develop, and retain the right talent in the organization to grow it. This is the reason why I wrote this book.

If you run an SMB, sit on the leadership team of an SMB, private equity backed firm, consultant or work with them as an investor or service provider to companies this size, this book is for you. It will equip you with the tools to elevate your HR practices or those of the companies you work with. This is crucial because your employees are essential for your company's success. This book will help you get better at hiring, developing, and retaining your precious human resources, your employees.

Think about the difference between a ship and a speed boat. The ship is very stable but can't change course or adapt quickly. A speed boat can change speed and direction within seconds. SMBs can change and adapt within days or weeks, whereas a Fortune 500 can't.

This book is broken down into short chapters on the different major building blocks within the HR function that you need to focus on. Your employees are all different and come from very different backgrounds and experiences. The key to run a successful business is to lead with a people strategy that aligns with your business strategy. If your business is growing, transforming, or acquiring other businesses, you need a people strategy to address those issues proactively vs. reactively.

Each chapter in this book covers a specific HR topic or process and will have a Case Study or Story that gives specific client examples of an actual HR problem that I helped a company solve after I started HR Catalyst in 2013. The case studies will be shown at the beginning of the chapter. Even if you need help with only one area of HR, I recommend reading the entire book. I guarantee you'll learn many actionable ideas and processes along the way that will help you run a better business or nonprofit. If you can implement even a handful of ideas discussed here, you'll create significant revenue opportunities, and cost savings for your business.

Enjoy the book! It will help improve the HR or employee side of your business.

Chapter One

Workforce Challenges

The workforce is quickly being populated with Gen Zers (born 1997–2012) and millennials (born 1981–1996), currently about 54% of the workforce. Younger employees want to clearly understand the company's mission as well as how their role contributes to that mission. They are looking for more than a job and a paycheck. They want to work for a company that truly cares about them as a person, not just an employee. Their definition of work-life balance is much different than Gen X employees or baby boomers.

Abraham Maslow was a twentieth-century psychologist who came up with a hierarchy of needs. At the base, our needs are for food, water, shelter—things we need to survive. As those needs are met, we have more complex needs. Gen Zers and millennials have more of these basic needs met, so they want more from their work experience. They want love, belonging, and esteem as seen in Maslow's hierarchy below.

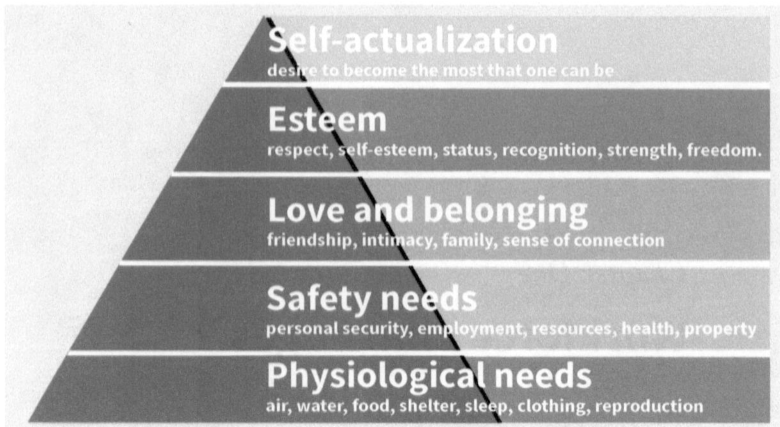

Many companies run by baby boomers and Gen Xers don't understand what younger employees want in a career, and, in some cases, they truly don't care what they want. They will continue to follow their established methods and if younger employees are not comfortable with this, too bad. Companies that struggle to hire new talent tend to hire the wrong people or haven't clearly defined the right employee profile. More to come on that later.

The irony is the largest single expense in a company are the HR-related costs. Think about it. Payroll, benefits, taxes, and training are every company's biggest expense. HR involves every employee. SMBs usually have few resources focused on hiring and selection, employee retention, developing and maintaining a healthy company culture, leadership development, succession planning, and more. The most valuable component of any business—the people—are often an afterthought.

If you lose an employee, you just hire another one to take their role. It's that simple, right? Wrong. *The average cost of hiring an employee is currently between $7,000 to $10,000 per hire.* For manager and executive level positions, the cost is much higher.

The cost for a company with 20 percent employee turnover annually is astronomical. For a company with one hundred employees, that could be $200,000 a year just on turnover expenses. If you can lower that turnover rate to 5–8 percent annually, you could save tens of thousands of dollars just in recruiting time and cost. That number does not include the ramp-up time to get an employee fully productive, which could take three to six months or longer, depending on their job. By being more intentional about employee onboarding and overall employee experience once they are hired, you can lower your turnover rate.

Your employees are your most important asset. If you don't hire the right employees in the right position, give them the right training, keep them engaged and excited about the work they are doing, where would that leave you?

Your fixed assets, like your equipment, machinery, or fleet vehicles don't have a choice about where they work. Your employees, on the other hand, *choose* where they work and whether they will return to work tomorrow. As a business owner or leader, it is paramount for you to create the culture and environment that motivates your employees to *want* to come to work each day, one that truly engages them in their work and positions them to do it to the best of their ability.

In my experience, most SMBs handle their HR issues reactively rather than proactively. They deal with a problem with an employee during or after a crisis occurs. Once that issue is fixed they go back to business as usual, ignoring the root cause of the employee issue. I call this the whack a mole theory of management.

Chances are, until you address the root cause of the issue, you will continue to "whack" the "mole" back into the hole over and over again. You may become very good at playing the game, but your employee issues will continue to pop up. I challenge you to quit playing whack a mole and develop a better solution that solves the root cause.

The Secret Sauce of any Company

Most successful organizations establish core processes for all major functions within the company, extending beyond just human resources. Sales, accounting, marketing, operations, quality, safety, they all require processes that are documented and followed consistently.

During the 2000s I worked for PepsiCo, a Fortune 50 company with over 300,000 employees globally. They are highly successful and enjoy a truly great culture. Why is PepsiCo so successful? Because they follow core processes for everything they do, including HR. Despite hiring employees across the globe, they still follow a similar HR process for hiring. It may vary slightly by country, but it is still fundamentally the same.

Understanding and building core HR processes are important to companies whether you have 50 employees or 50,000 employees. Every company needs foundational and scalable HR processes to successfully grow. Like every other function within the company, it's best to build those processes early in the company's formation. It's like building a house. Without a solid foundation and quality framing, the house will have constant issues.

Core HR Processes

- Selection and hiring
- Onboarding
- Offboarding
- Annual reviews
- Compensation determination
- Benefit package design and enrollment
- Disciplinary process
- Payroll and benefits administration
- Internal communications
- Leadership development
- Employee engagement
- Change management
- Succession planning

The list shown here is not all-encompassing, but it covers the major processes.

As I've explained, your employees are your most important asset, and the cost of your employees is around 50–75 percent of the overall cost of your business regardless of industry. These costs include pay, health benefits, PTO or vacation, bonuses, profit sharing, and 401K match (if offered). Your employee costs require a significant amount of money. Make sure you take care of them throughout the hiring and onboarding process and all touchpoints throughout their tenure, whether that's for three years or thirty years.

Never take your employees for granted. I cringe when I hear leaders of companies say that they have an annual turnover rate of 20, 30, even 40 percent, and it's taken for granted. In those cases, I ask why? Why do employees leave the company? Do they share similar reasons for their departure?

Do you conduct exit interviews with employees and ask them why they are leaving your company? Some turnover is expected, especially in certain industries like hospitality. There are also companies in high-turnover industries that boast a much lower turnover rate than the industry standard. Why do they have a low turnover rate compared to their competitors? Because they focus on hiring the right people and taking care of them, not giving up and saying that our industry has high turnover and there is nothing that we can do about it. They create a healthy company culture which we will look at in the next chapter.

Chapter Two

Company Culture

We worked with a manufacturing company several years ago that builds high-end custom cabinetry, trim, and staircases for new residential homes. When we started consulting for them, they didn't have a mission statement or set of core values that defined the company's culture and who they were both internally and externally. The mission statement and core values are what sets the tone of a company's culture. We worked with the owners, leaders, and their customers, who are home builders, to clearly define the mission statement and core values.

The process focused on the key differentiators that separated them from their competitors. By going through this process, we helped them determine why they exist, their mission, and what core values define them as a business. Below you will see the results on how creating these critical items gave them clarity and laser focus. This creates not only a better place to work, but it also financially improves both top and bottom line. In addition, it clearly defines the types of customers they want to work with since not every customer is a good customer.

By clearly defining their culture, they increased employee engagement and productivity. A more engaged employee is more productive. Gallup research finds that engaged teams are 23 percent more profitable and companies with strong cultures often see turnover rates up to 40 percent lower than competitors.[1]

We also helped them change their hiring process so they could find employees who best fit the company culture. This lowered their employee turnover rate. The impact has saved the company thousands of dollars annually in hiring and new employee training costs.

The financial impact was also very positive for them. After a few years, when their revenue growth was in the single digits, their profitability landed in the double digits. That is a sign of a well-run company. Our work to help them clearly define their culture made a positive impact quickly and will continue to do so for years to come.

Clearly, investing in company culture is a strategic imperative, creating better employee experience and engagement levels which lead to better financial performance and sustainable growth.

Every company has a culture. Who defines the company culture? Is it the owners, the CEO, the president of the company, or the employees? My response is that culture needs to be defined by the CEO or president and the leadership team. The culture needs to be intentional and leadership driven. If you let the employees define the culture it is like letting the prisoners run the prison. Of course, I'm not saying your employees are prisoners, but you get the gist here.

Your company culture is a strategic differentiator from your competition. Let that sink in for a minute. Everything else your company does can be replicated by your competitors. For this reason, it is important that you focus on your company culture. Regardless of company size, an intentional leadership-driven culture is critically important to the long-term success of your company.

A set of shared core values, beliefs, and behaviors shape how employees interact with each other and the outside world. In fact, over time, companies with strong cultures tend to outperform those with weak ones in terms of revenue, customer loyalty, and profitability. Zappos is a great example of this. Zappos follows the Holacracy model, a model that distributes "power throughout the organization, and if done properly it gives individuals and teams more freedom to self-manage." Another famous thing that Zappos does is during their onboarding process, they will pay people two thousand dollars to quit. If you don't like your job in the first month, they will pay you to quit, no questions asked. They believe that if you're not fully committed to the brand, they don't want you to stay long-term.[2]

Key drivers for how companies with great cultures like Zappos financially outperform their peers include:

- productivity and execution (higher employee engagement)
- decision making quality (allowing for robust debate to get to better results)
- cost of human capital (lower employee turnover rates)
- risk management and compliance (better leadership driving to better employee management)

In 2022, when global organizational consulting firm Korn Ferry surveyed more than fifteen thousand executives worldwide as part of its World's Most Admired Companies Research, two-thirds of those surveyed said they felt culture accounted for more than 30 percent of the market value of their respective organizations. A Harvard Business Review study found that companies with strong cultures saw revenues increase over a ten-year period by four times as much as those with weaker cultures.

A key point to remember is that a company culture can be negative too. There are many examples where owners or executives lose sight of why the company exists. In some cases greed, ego, or arrogance get in the way of rational thinking and doing the right thing for employees. The classic real-life example here is Enron. A Houston-based energy trading and utilities corporation, Enron had an aggressive, win-at-all-costs company culture that prized short-term profits and personal gain over ethics and transparency. Executives discouraged dissent, rewarded risky behavior, and normalized deception, leading to massive accounting fraud, investor betrayal, bankruptcy in 2001, and collapse. Enron even used a very non-traditional accounting method called mark-to-market to be able to fraudulently hide its issues from both employees and outside auditors.

A company with a strong positive culture, on the other hand, is very resilient to major internal or external headwinds. In 1982, seven people died after taking Extra Strength Tylenol. The issue was isolated in an area of Chicago, where investigators discovered that someone tampered with Tylenol containers, lacing them with potassium cyanide. Tylenol was a subsidiary of Johnson & Johnson company, a huge company manufacturing all types of healthcare products.

To get through the scandal, the executives leaned on the company Credo considered to be their core values:

- **Prioritizing Public Safety:** Placing patient well-being over financial profit, illustrated by the decision to recall all products in 1982.
- **Quality and Trust:** Ensuring products are of high quality and maintaining public trust.
- **Responsibility to Community:** Acting as good citizens, supporting health and education.
- **Continuous Improvement/Innovation:** Investing in research and developing new ideas for the future.

Given what they called their moral compass, Tylenol removed all of the products in the Chicago area. To its credit, the company took an active role with the media. It issued mass warnings and immediately called for a massive recall of the more than 31 million bottles of Tylenol in circulation. This caused the company to lose millions of dollars in revenue and greatly impacted the stock price and reputation of the iconic brand for a period.

As a result, sweeping changes were made in the entire over-the-counter (OTC) drug industry to ensure product safety. Those changes were made in the early 1980s, and to my knowledge there hasn't been a major safety issue like this one with an OTC drug since.

According to the Drucker Institute's (a nonprofit organization devoted to the improvement of management practices) Peter Drucker, is quoted as saying, "culture—no matter how defined—is singularly persistent." This quote has morphed into the popular expression "culture eats strategy for breakfast." This saying reflects that company culture outlasts strategic planning.

Companies with a strong, healthy culture tend to have an easier time recruiting, and in many cases applicants contact *them* about openings. This can lead to a pipeline of talented people who apply to work for the company. Once the employee is hired, they want to stay with you.

According to Bureau of Labor and Statistics (BLS.gov study) in April 2025, the median employee tenure is around 3.5 years. Companies with a strong culture have a much higher tenure rate, whereby an employee stays with them for a longer period of time. That fact increases your productivity and profitability. Companies with a weak or toxic culture have a higher turnover rate. This is why a strong culture is so important.

Employees leave their company for a variety of reasons. Some leave because they don't trust or respect their boss. This continues to be one of the top three reasons why employees leave a company. Others leave because they're not happy in the role they've been assigned or the overall work environment. But others leave simply because they don't feel like the role is the right fit for them and their personal career growth.

Employees want to be a part of something bigger than themselves; they want to participate in a growing and thriving organization with a strong culture. When you create and foster this type of culture within your workforce, you're able to better retain employees by providing them with opportunities for advancement, empowerment, and transparency as well as helping them feel more connected to the company's vision, mission, and core values

Better Employee Health

One less obvious benefit of a strong organizational culture is it helps employees lead healthier lives. In fact, studies have shown that people who work for companies with strong cultures are more likely to be active and eat healthier than those who don't.

This is partly due to workplace activities like walking or stand-up meetings, standing desks, and healthy break opportunities that help break down barriers between employees and encourage socializing. It also means that you can use your company culture to encourage your employees to get on board with fitness programs or health initiatives (which will ultimately benefit them both physically and mentally). A healthy employee also reduces the level of employee absenteeism and can reduce the rates for health insurance premiums.

In addition to helping improve their own health, employees with healthy habits are also better equipped to contribute effectively toward the success of their organization—which makes this benefit one that goes beyond individual well-being. This impacts the company financially as well.

Reputation

A strong organizational culture can help you build a positive reputation and increase customer loyalty. People admire companies such as Apple, Patagonia, Ritz Carlton, Zappos, and Nike for their strong, positive culture. Your brand reputation is a key factor in building customer loyalty and can even attract new customers to your business. For instance, if you have a great reputation for providing excellent customer service, people will be more likely to choose your business over another one that doesn't offer the same high-quality customer service.

But what happens when something goes wrong? Your poor employee performance or behavior could tarnish your company's reputation by creating negative experiences for customers and other stakeholders. A strong organizational culture can help prevent this from happening by keeping employees accountable for their actions, so they don't make mistakes that hurt the company's image among clients or partners.

Communication

A strong culture leads to better communication which leads to improved productivity. As you can see, the benefits of this approach are many. Employees of companies with a strong culture of regular and transparent communication feel valued, properly informed, and respected at work and therefore feel motivated to give their best efforts. Companies where communication—especially top-down communication—is not good suffer from poor morale.

When employees work together collaboratively on projects or tasks, they share information more freely and openly because they trust each other. This makes it easier for them to communicate with one another about any changes in process or procedure that may need attention before implementation. This can help avoid costly mistakes that could otherwise occur when changes are implemented without sufficient advanced planning and save money for your company in the long run!

As you can see there are many reasons why the executive team of an organization need to make it a priority to have a leadership driven culture.

Chapter Three

Recruiting

We consulted twice in the last decade with a manufacturing company that struggled to find quality talent because their recruiting process was inconsistent and the time to fill a role (TTF in HR lingo) often surpassed the industry standard of forty-five days, sometimes even taking longer than sixty days. The TTF is defined as the amount of time from the beginning of the recruitment process to when an offer is made and accepted by the candidate.

This particular company did not have a standard set of interview questions for their job applicants. They did use a hiring assessment, but they didn't use it effectively, and the HR department made the hire without the managers' input. The results were mediocre with higher turnover costs since many new employees couldn't do the job effectively and either resigned or were terminated in the first year of employment. That led to situations where projects were behind schedule and revenue goals ultimately were not met. The entire hiring and selection process needed to be revamped.

Once the issues were clearly identified, leadership calculated the financial impact the subpar hiring had on the business. The annual costs in lost productivity, high turnover rate, and retraining new hires were estimated at between $400,000 and $600,000 for a company with less than $100 million in revenue. Once we explained the monetary impact, the executive team started working on a fix.

We helped the client create structured interview templates for core roles that were hired frequently. We also helped them clearly identify ownership in the hiring process itself—who owns what and when—so there weren't breakdowns in the process itself. Given the company's size at the time (fewer than three hundred employees), a full-time recruiter didn't make financial sense for them, so we identified an outsourced recruiting solution. Lastly, managers were held accountable to conduct interviews in a timely manner once ideal candidates were identified.

The implemented changes improved the entire process drastically. Better candidates were identified, the average time to fill dropped to around forty-five days per hire, and the turnover rate went from close to 20 percent to 12 percent annually. The estimated annual cost savings was between $150,000 and $300,000, directly impacting profitability. The impact was significant from both an employee and financial perspective.

Investing in a robust recruiting process is a strategic decision that yields significant returns. From improving the quality of the candidates and reducing costs to strengthening the employer brand, the benefits are far reaching. Ultimately, organizations that prioritize effective recruiting are better positioned to achieve their goals, adapt to change, and maintain a sustainable competitive advantage.

There are several actionable steps to select and hire the right talent for your business. In this chapter we are going to discuss critical components to this process.

First, make sure the job description is accurate for the position. Often a job description hasn't been updated in years, and the job description is no longer accurate for the current job requirements. Before you begin looking for any new employees, confirm with the hiring manager that the job description is still accurate and requires the core skills and competencies listed for the position. You also need to confirm the minimum years of experience, education level, and any specific experience needed to be considered. It's not uncommon to discover after the job is posted and you are interviewing candidates, that you are fishing in the wrong pond for people with core skills and competencies required for an obsolete job description. When this occurs everyone is frustrated.

Next, a job description does not equal a job posting. If you are using job boards like Indeed, LinkedIn, and Zip Recruiter, you need to have a job posting that reads more like a marketing piece rather than something that is dry and boring. You need to clearly show why the "buyer" or candidate should apply for your position versus the fifty other similar positions that are posted on job boards that day. This is especially true for standard roles such as junior or mid-level accounting, HR, customer service, and sales and marketing positions. A well-written job post separates you from the pack. Describe what makes your company unique, discuss the pay range for the position, unique benefits you offer, career growth opportunities, and remote or hybrid work options is they exist.

Here are a few great tips from a recent LinkedIn post.

- Remember that less is more, shorter job posts will receive more applicants
- Focus on what matters, the majority of candidates say the salary range is the most important part of the job posting
- Save culture for later, that can be discussed during the interview process itself
- Keep it real, be honest and transparent in your job post
- Be mindful of the words you use, keep it gender neutral
- Promote job posts on Mondays: more than half of all applicants apply for jobs early in the week[1]

Referral Program

Another key to think about is having an effective employee referral program to get your employees to help fill open positions. Chances are that your employees know people who may want to join your company. Pay well for employee referrals bonuses. We see companies pay $250 to $500 for an employee referral. After taxes and being paid out in several payments, that is not much of an incentive. Employee referrals that are $1,000, $2,500, and even $10,000 are not uncommon nowadays. Of course, there are many factors that go into the right amount to pay, but if you are hiring aggressively now, your existing employees can be your best recruiters. Make sure you use the employee referral program effectively as part of your overall recruitment process.

Core Value Alignment

Make sure you integrate your company's core values into the hiring and selection process. First off, make sure you have a consistent set of interview questions you ask all candidates. If you have five managers interviewing for the same role and they use totally different interview questions, you have no consistency in the process. It's like comparing apples, oranges, and bananas, they are all fruit, but they are very different fruits. Remember, the selection process is like any other business process, make sure it's consistent among anyone who interviews to ensure you have consistent feedback and you're using the same hiring lens to assess candidates. The reason to specifically talk about your core values in the interview process is to look for employees who will be a good culture fit for your company.

Many candidates may be a great technical fit for the company, but they are not a good cultural fit. In many cases, employees leave a company or are managed out because they don't fit the culture. It's like a friend who is socially awkward or says improper things at a dinner party you're hosting. It is awkward for everyone. People who don't fit your cultural norms are swimming upstream much of the time. Your culture should be strong enough that those employees will be rejected like a person who receives a kidney that isn't a perfect match.

We have seen too many technically good employees leave the company quickly or are asked to leave if they aren't good cultural fits. I saw that in my own career. I worked for a great company, but it wasn't an ideal cultural fit. The culture was not brought up during the interview process. I should have asked more about it but I didn't. I decided to leave that company before I hit my one-year anniversary.

Employee Brand

Have a strong employee brand. Your employee brand is what makes your employees unique and appear to be very similar in many ways. Certain people are attracted to your company for certain reasons. When you have a strong employer brand, you often don't have to recruit many employees because people want to work for your company and are trying to get in the door with you.

TalentBrand.org is a volunteer-led professional community and organization for recruitment marketers and employer branding professionals to network and share resources. According to TalentBrand, your talent brand is "the honest story of life as an employee inside your organization, as told by the employees in parallel with the company." That's a great quote. Don't oversell your company; be genuine and honest with candidates. They'll appreciate that from you during the recruiting process.

A strong employer brand is critical for selling the company to candidates interviewing with you. Of course, you need to be sincere here. If you don't offer the best benefits package, don't tell candidates you have a great benefits package. That is disingenuous and they will find out. That can do your company more harm than good. It can also lead to more questions from a new employee who might be thinking *What else didn't they tell me about during the interview?*

Explain to all candidates the great benefits your company offers. Good candidates will typically receive several quality job offers to consider. Why should this candidate work for your company? The hiring process is very similar to the sales process. The sale occurs when the ideal candidate accepts your job offer. Your company brand might differentiate your company from the others.

Post Internally/Succession Planning

Posting positions internally first is a good practice, especially for roles that offer career development or promotional opportunities. I recommend posting the position internally for one week before posting externally. If you don't post these positions internally first, this can come back to bite you. The hiring manager may assume no one in the company is interested or qualified without knowing the true internal interest in the position. Additionally, the hiring manager may be unaware of the previous experience or unknown qualifications of their employees. Not only does this have a negative impact on your workforce, but it can also stagnant employee career growth, lower employee engagement, and possibly create retention issues.

In probably 90 percent of the hiring situations, posting a role internally first makes total business sense. You want to allow internal candidates the first chance to interview, since they are already a known quantity compared to someone from the external market. Posting internally allows employees to grow and progress in their career. One of the top five reasons why employees leave a company is that they see no career growth for themselves. This is very true in the younger workforce, those under thirty-five years old. They are quickly becoming the largest contingent of the workforce as more baby boomers retire. The average employee tenure in the U.S. in 2025 was around four years according to McLean and Company, an HR Research and consulting firm. Remember that's an average, employees fifty-five and above average almost ten years tenure, while employees in their twenties average around 2.3 years tenure.

The workforce still has remote and/or hybrid workers, but that shift has stabilized with many companies bringing employees back into the office. Employee loyalty and possibly tenure likely will change. In many cases, employees are not as loyal to a company, but are loyal to their profession and the type of work they'll be doing. This is true with tech and research and development companies where employees want to work for employers with the most cutting edge or "coolest" technology.

As many baby boomer senior leaders move into retirement, internally promoting talent is critical in succession planning. There must be internal systems to move high-potential employees into bigger and more complex roles. Remember, recruitment can be both external and internal. A good internal recruitment strategy for promotional opportunities is directly correlated to employee retention, especially with top performers. If they don't see career growth and both lateral and vertical movement opportunities, the likelihood of them updating their resumes to seeking employment elsewhere is much greater.

Another great resource in today's recruiting environment is social media. To be competitive in your recruiting efforts make sure your company website has a career page to clearly show what positions are currently open. In some cases, if you have a position(s) that has a high turnover rate, you should keep the position on your career page.

All positions should be posted on social media. For mid-level management positions, post on LinkedIn, Facebook, and even X (formerly) Twitter. For hourly roles consider even posting on Craigslist. For executive positions, look into Ladders and Experteer. In many cases, you can use these recruiting tools for no cost or low cost, and they can be highly effective. You need to have many effective tools to recruit in today's competitive world of looking for great candidates for your company. The more you think about having a multi-pronged recruiting strategy the better. If candidates can find you in many different ways, that's a good thing.

Develop Recruiting Metrics

Lastly, create metrics around the recruitment function in your company. Depending on your company's size, you may spend a significant amount of money in your recruiting function itself or in your outsourced recruiting function or RPO (recruitment process outsourcing). If you work for a high growth company, you may be spending $100,000 plus annually on recruiting efforts. That's the hard cost. The soft cost is the time spent interviewing candidates by your HR team and managers. That said, make sure you have good metrics to measure the ROI (return on investment) on your recruiting efforts. In today's world, the recruiting function is really a marketing function that's housed in HR.

If you are a middle-market company (less than one thousand employees), you may not have the bandwidth to create and measure all these metrics. Pick the top three or four and measure them consistently.

Hiring manager satisfaction

Hiring manager satisfaction measures the quality of hire. Use surveys to gauge how hiring managers feel about new team members. Ask them questions about how satisfied they are with the new hire, such as

- How satisfied are you with the candidates?
- How clear was the communication with your recruiter?
- How helpful was your recruiter?
- How likely are you to work with this recruiter again?

Consider resources like the talent experience solutions company Survale to help you craft questions for internal surveys.

Cost Per Hire

The cost per hire metric is used by recruiting staff to determine how much money the company spends hiring a new employee. This metric can help identify how many new employees can be hired within a given fiscal year based on your company's budget. It can also be an avenue to reduce costs on the annual budget. Businesses with high employee turnover should be especially careful about their cost per hire.

To calculate this recruiting metric, add your total internal and external recruiting costs for a given time frame and divide them by the number of employees hired during that same time.

Time to Hire

The time to hire, or time to fill metric tells you how long the hiring process takes. It can be used to evaluate the level of productivity among your recruiting staff and the effectiveness of your recruiting strategies. This metric is especially important if you're losing key employees faster than you've been able to replace them.

To calculate the time to hire subtract the number of days passed between posting an open position and filling it. Average time to hire among several openings can also be calculated by adding the specific times to hire for each and then dividing the sum total of them by the number of roles.

Offer Acceptance Rate

The offer acceptance rate is the percentage of candidates who accept your job offer. This metric can be used to determine the success rate of recruitment tactics in attracting and securing talented professionals who say yes to your company's job offer. If your calculations show an initial high interest, but low acceptance, you should consider what factors might be causing candidates to decline a job at your company.

To calculate the offer acceptance rate simply divide the number of accepted job offers by the total number of jobs that were offered during the same period of time. The percentage outcome of this represents how likely candidates are to accept your job openings.

New Hire Turnover Rate

A new hire turnover rate is the percentage of new employees who resign within a certain time frame. It can be used to measure turnover during arbitrary periods of time such as a month or several months. If the turnover rate is high, consider reviewing exit interview documents with your human resources department to understand what factors led to employees' quick departures.

Calculate new hire turnover by dividing the number of departures during a certain time by the number of people hired during the same time. Multiply the result by 100 for a percentage. You can set the time frames at one month, three months, six months or any range you like.

Candidates Per Hire

The candidates per hire metric is one of the key measurements of the effectiveness of your recruitment process. It's derived from the number of candidates interviewed in order to fill the position. Improving this metric can help you save time on interviews and better align hiring criteria with potential candidates. Candidates per hire also measures how well your recruiters and hiring managers are performing. Ideally, it should be no more than four or five.

Candidate Callback Rate

Another important recruitment metric is the candidate callback rate. It measures the number of candidates your organization's recruiters contacted compared to the number of candidates who responded. For example, if your company contacts a dozen candidates with an offer and requests that they reply, but only one does, this is a poor callback ratio.

The candidate callback ratio also measures the effectiveness of your recruiting. This metric allows you to observe the performance of each recruiting method (email, phone, or other means) so you can adjust your pitch to increase your effectiveness.

Candidate Experience

Also known as net performer score, the candidate experience metric attempts to quantify how a candidate perceives their recruiting experience with your organization. This qualifies your recruiting tactics from an external viewpoint.

To determine the candidate experience ask your candidates to score the performance of your recruiting across several metrics, such as responsiveness, interview competence, communication skills, and courtesy. The result is an overall score of your own hiring managers as perceived by new or potential employees.

Sourcing Channel Effectiveness

Sourcing channel effectiveness measures the extent that each sourcing channels contributes to your overall hiring process. The successful recruitment metrics you derive from each channel reveals which channels need to be optimized. Examples of sourcing channels include email outreach campaigns, recruitment ads, social networks, and personal contacts.

To quantify this metric count how many successful candidates each channel has generated over an equal number of outreach attempts per channel. A given time frame might also be used as a measurement for all channels, but you should control for the possibility that not all channels are used with the same frequency.

Sourcing Channel Cost

Related to sourcing channel effectiveness is sourcing channel cost. This measures your sourcing channels costs in labor expenses, ad spend, or other monetary outlays per successful candidate. It is calculated by adding the cost of sourcing platform, such as social media ads, during a designated time frame divided by candidates hired during the same time.

Retention Rate

Employee retention rate is one of the more important key performance indicators (KPIs) that your organization should monitor. It measures your ability to keep employees. High employee turnover is a sign that something isn't working well inside your organization or that your hiring process needs to be improved.

Retention rate can be measured by dividing the total number of employees who stayed for an entire measurement of time by the total number of employees at the start of that time frame.

Fill Rate

Your organization's fill rate is an interesting recruiting metric for deciding if you should use your organization's recruiting process to find new candidates or rely on an external agency. By assigning an equal number of positions to fill to both your internal hiring team and a recruiting service and by giving both the same fixed period of time to fill them, you can measure how well each performs.

This metric is calculated by diving the total number of jobs filled by the total number of jobs assigned.

Application Completion Rate

The application completion rate measures the performance and quality of your job application process and platforms. This performance metric is based on the number of candidate engagements with your application platforms or systems compared to the number of fully completed applications. For example, a faulty online application form that frequently crashes might be the cause of a low application completion rate.

This metric can be measured by dividing the number of submitted applications by the total number of applications that were started and then multiply by 100 for a percentage.

Selection Ratio

The selection ratio measures the competitiveness of your open job offerings on the wider market. If your open positions consistently generate high volumes of applicants relative to the number of people you hire per position it indicates that either those positions or employment with your organization are highly sought after.

The selection ratio can be calculated by dividing the number of candidates you hired by all the applicants for a specific position. If you're measuring the selection ratio for multiple positions, then divide the total number of hired candidates by the total number of applications for all positions.

In summary, recruiting is a key component in any well-run company. For SMBs, focus on three to four recruiting metrics that you can easily track and are meaningful for managers to understand. Every company regardless of size spends a tremendous amount of time and money recruiting, especially if you are growing. Making sure your recruiting spend is used wisely and adjust it if you need to get the most bang for your buck. The next chapter dives into the importance of a comprehensive onboarding process for your new employees. Make sure you nurture your valuable new hire to make a great impression once they join the business.

Chapter Four

Onboarding

Over the last several years, we have been consulting for a company that works in the construction equipment industry. Their annual employee turnover rate was between 20 and 30 percent depending on the role.

We discovered most employees were leaving within their first twelve to twenty-four months of employment. Training costs to fully assimilate employees surpassed tens of thousands of dollars in the first six months. Managers were often not hiring ideal candidates; they were filling positions with C players simply to fill the role quickly.

When we started working with the client, we discovered they had virtually no onboarding process. The company had multiple locations and hadn't established a cohesive process. Employee onboarding differed greatly by location. Working with internal full-time employees, we helped them create a consistent onboarding process.

When it comes to your employees, the key is to hire slow and fire fast. We'll address the "fire fast" part of that saying later in the book. Many candidates can interview very well, but then fall significantly short once they begin the job. Many studies show that over 30 percent of job candidates embellish their resumes and state they possess certain skill sets which they do not have. A good onboarding process will quickly determine if a new hire has the skills they stated on their resume.

A good onboarding process goes beyond tasks and procedures; it actively encourages social integration. The company already knew they had a major challenge with employee turnover; we helped them build a framework to address the onboarding issue and train managers how to interview and onboard employees better. We helped them focus on integrating the employee into the existing team, not only focusing on getting them up to speed on their job.

The result: employee turnover rate decreased.

Many organizations confuse employee onboarding with orientation and assume it is administrative rather than strategic. Onboarding is more than completing the necessary paperwork and other routine tasks for each new employee. This is the smaller and lesser part of onboarding which is a comprehensive process involving management and other employees that can last up to twelve months.

The process outlined below applies to both office-based, field-based, and remote employees. Remote onboarding differs slightly but shares the same basic process. With virtual meeting technology and instant messaging or chat software available, it's rather simple to stay connected with your new hires whether working remotely or in the office.

What is Employee Onboarding?

Employee onboarding is the key transitional period of assimilating a new hire to the organization's values, culture, systems, and processes and giving them the tools and information needed to become a productive member of the team. Society for HR Management (SHRM) employee onboarding guide says, "onboarding is the process of helping new hires adjust to social and performance aspects of their new jobs quickly and smoothly."[1]

In many organizations, however, the onboarding process is almost nonexistent and doesn't help new hires acclimate or integrate into the organization or their roles within it and employees are left to figure that out on their own. Some eventually will, but others will feel they made a mistake by joining your team and will seek employment elsewhere. The sink or swim strategy in which new employees often struggle to figure out what is expected of their role and a lack of clear understanding of company norms and their new workplace only leads to frustration for employees and managers alike and an endless stream of turnover.

Proper Onboarding = Employee Retention

Onboarding new hires at an organization should be a strategic process that lasts at least twelve weeks and can be as long as one year because how employers handle the first few days and months of a new employee's experience is crucial to ensuring high retention. According to Zavvy.io, a German-based employee enablement platform that streamlines onboarding, performance management, and career development, half of all senior outside hires fail within eighteen months in a new position, and half of all hourly workers leave new jobs within the first 120 days. Research by Brandon Hall Group found that organizations with a strong onboarding process improve new hire retention by 82 percent and productivity by over 70 percent. According to *Inc. Magazine*, the chance of an employee quitting is two to four times greater in the first year of employment without an effective onboarding process. On average, it costs $7000–$10,000 to bring on one employee. That's an average, of course, so it includes employees who make $18 per hour and $100,000+ a year. If your workforce is primarily hourly workers, the cost of turnover becomes staggering and can hinder a company's growth significantly. Finding the best candidates for positions in your organization is only part of building an effective team.[2]

The process of onboarding new employees can be one of the most critical factors in ensuring recently hired talent will become productive and engaged workers. In many cases, when my firm starts working with a company, they have no onboarding process. We diligently work with them to resolve that weakness by helping them create a strong onboarding process that is refined over time.

Starting Your Onboarding Process

Before implementing a formal onboarding program, companies should answer several important questions to achieve buy-in from other employees and the management team:

- When will onboarding start?
- How long will it last?
- What impression do you want new hires to walk away with at the end of the first day?

- What do new employees need to know about the culture and work environment?
- What role will HR play in the process? What about direct managers and coworkers?
- What kind of goals do you want to set for new employees?
- How will you gather feedback on the program and measure its success?

Once these questions have been answered, the HR and management team can devise a plan of action to help new employees quickly assimilate company policies and workflow while getting fully acquainted with the organization's culture.

Before the First Day

Employee preboarding is important as it sets the stage for what comes next and shows a new hire that they have made the right choice in selecting your company as a place of employment. Consider this the first impression of the company, prior to day one start date. Preboarding should include a welcome email to your new hire, sharing excitement to have them on the team and providing some details around next steps. This may include:

- Details for first day success (building entry details, arrival time, itinerary of the day)
- A link to complete new hire paperwork, ideally online
- A mentor/buddy introduction
- Team introduction
- Information including history of the business, team, core values, and culture
- Perhaps a swag bag with company gear sent to their home

- Request for technology preferences (standing desk, Mac vs. PC, etc.) if that's an option to consider

The First Few Weeks and Months

It's important for you to schedule a weekly check-in for the first four to six weeks to ensure new employees are comfortable, engaged and settling into their roles. The weekly check-in may need to be only fifteen minutes if everything is going well. Reviewing and giving thoughtful feedback on your new hire's early contributions are important during the onboarding process. This also gives the manager a chance to answer any questions they have. Then you can begin reducing the number of check-ins after a month or two depending on the new hire's progress.

During the onboarding process, you are making sure you made a good hiring decision. The interview process is never 100 percent accurate; it doesn't matter how well you did it. I wish I had a 100 percent foolproof interview process. If I did, I would be quite rich. A good onboarding process will raise red flags if the person is not a good fit for the role. Then you can quickly assess whether they are going to work out long term or not and take the appropriate action.

If you aren't communicating what new hires are supposed to be doing and arming them with the tools to do it properly, you're setting them up to fail. You don't want to inundate your new hires with too much information. While it's important to get your new hire ramped up and productive quickly, you also need to make sure you provide on-the-job training in a manageable flow. That's why the new employee should have realistic goals for the first thirty, sixty, and ninety days to track their progress and see where they might be having issues in their performance. This is especially important for positions that have naturally higher turnover than other positions. If it appears the new employee cannot hit realistic goals during the onboarding period, then you may need to formalize corrective action steps to exit the employee.

It is important for new hires to have a mentor during the onboarding period and perhaps longer. Surveys overwhelmingly show that having a buddy or mentor at work is very important when getting started. According to a 2015 Aberdeen report high-performing organizations are nearly two and a half times more likely than lower-performing employers to assign a mentor or coach during the onboarding process.[3]

Mentoring programs can be as simple as assigning a new employee a go-to person or having a team of mentors available for any questions that might arise. The mentor should not be the new hire's boss. This is extremely important. In many cases, new employees are afraid to ask the boss a dumb question. Choose the design that best fits your company culture to help the new hire succeed.

The First 90 Days

Research and conventional wisdom suggests that employees get about ninety days to prove themselves in a new job. The faster new hires feel welcome and equipped for their jobs, the faster they will successfully contribute to the firm's mission and ramp up their productivity.

Gallup found that only 12 percent of employees strongly agree their organization does a great job of onboarding new employees. That means 88 percent *don't* believe their organizations do a great job of onboarding, which leaves a lot of room for improvement. You spend a considerable amount of time and money hiring the ideal candidate for your position so go the extra mile and create a robust onboarding process to significantly increase employee retention.

Strong employee onboarding programs extend up to ninety days to help new hires fully ramp. To do this, I suggest

- Weekly check-ins for the first month to recognize successes and identify areas where the new hire may need some additional help.
- Check-ins after thirty, sixty, and ninety days.
- Ongoing training and development.
- Mentor or buddy check-ins (once per week for the first month, once or twice per month thereafter). Remember the mentor does not replace the manager's role

The First Three to Six Months

It may be advisable to conduct another check-in between three and six months depending on the employee's performance and the complexity of the role. Unfortunately, only 15 percent of companies who conduct onboarding continue it after three months. Remember, nearly 90 percent of employees decide whether to stay or go within those first three to six months. You have a huge impact on that choice. Sometimes they just need to know that you sincerely care about them. This can go a long way toward building employee loyalty and trust. That's huge from a retention perspective.

The First Six to Twelve Months

Here are a few final, but very important thoughts for onboarding during the first six to twelve months of a new employee's journey. In fact, polling company Gallup finds that new team members typically take around twelve months to reach peak performance potential. This is especially true for roles that are highly complex.

During that timeframe, a good onboarding process helps employees understand their career path. One of the top reasons employees leave a company is that they don't see career growth or a long-term future with the company. As the average age of the workforce continues to lower; millennials and Gen Zers want to understand where they can go within the company. If they don't see a bright future with you, they may decide to go somewhere else where they think a better career path exists.

Depending on the company, make sure they understand that career progression can equal both vertical and lateral moves. Employees need to gain breadth of knowledge across different functions to be better equipped for bigger jobs longer term. An employee's career journey is like chess more than checkers. They should be thinking strategically rather than one move at a time. Unfortunately, most people put more thought and research into buying their next car compared to what their career path should look like.

The Four Cs of Employee Onboarding

Here are the essentials of effective employee onboarding:

- *Compliance* is the lowest level and includes instructing employees about basic legal and policy-related rules and regulations.
- *Clarification* refers to ensuring that employees understand their new jobs and all related expectations. How well new hires understand their role is the most consistent predictor of job satisfaction and organizational commitment during the onboarding process.
- *Culture* is a broad category that includes providing employees with a sense of organizational norms, the processes, both formal and informal, for how they get their work done within the company.
- *Connection* refers to the vital interpersonal relationships and information networks that new employees must establish. New employees need to feel socially comfortable and accepted by their peers and superiors. Research has long found acceptance by peers to be an indicator of adjustment. Integration and connection in one's work group is positively related to commitment. Employees want to be part of a community. The more connected a new employees feels, the better the chance of their longevity with the company.

Here are some best onboarding practices to help make your program a success:

- Implement the basics *prior* to the new employee's first day on the job
- Make the first day on the job special
- Employ formal orientation programs
- Develop a written onboarding plan or process
- Make onboarding a joint effort between HR, the manager and employee
- Ensure your program is consistently implemented across the company
- Ensure the program is monitored over time
- Use technology to facilitate the process
- Use milestones, such as 30, 60, 90 and 120 days on the job, to check in on employee progress
- Engage stakeholders in planning the onboarding process
- Include key stakeholder meetings as part of the program
- Be crystal clear with new employees in terms of objectives, timelines, roles, and responsibilities

A successful onboarding process is a key part of any talent management strategy. With the high cost of recruiting, business leaders must understand that effectively integrating new hires into the organization is an important step to ensure their success. Understanding who owns the onboarding process as a whole and who controls various steps in the process is vital to onboarding success and sustainability over time. Simply writing down a formal plan will not help new employees succeed. The key is to engage important stakeholders and new employees in interactions that help them understand one another and how they interact over time. Effective onboarding will result in a faster learning curve for new hires, improved communication, and a more productive and engaged workforce. If this isn't a strong business case for having an excellent onboarding program, I'm not sure what would be.

Chapter Five

Talent Management

Talent management encompasses the full spectrum of activities related to recruiting, developing, engaging, and retaining employees. As companies strive to innovate, adapt, and grow, the ability to attract, retain, and develop top talent has become a strategic imperative.

Over several years, I have worked with a transportation and logistics company, supporting them with strategic HR systems and processes. We built a strong talent management system throughout different facets of the organization. We focused on everything concerning the employee journey or life cycle with the company. The company didn't really have a systematic way of looking at every facet of managing their talent effectively. We worked with them to build a detailed onboarding process, reviewed external compensation benchmarking annually on many positions, conducted succession planning on all or most of the organization annually and finally, we conducted leadership development for the entry and mid-level leaders company wide. The CEO knew that effective talent management is no longer a luxury; it is a necessity for businesses seeking to maintain a competitive edge. We focused on the following:

- Creating a comprehensive onboarding process for each position
- Hiring outside talent to fill strategic leadership gaps
- Growing and retaining talent throughout the organization
- Giving employees total compensation statements to show the entire dollars spent for each employee

The Bottom-Line Impact of Talent Management

A well-designed talent management strategy delivers the following benefits:

- **Improved Recruitment and Retention:** By leveraging employer branding, targeted sourcing, and effective onboarding, organizations can attract and retain high-caliber talent.
- **Enhanced Employee Engagement:** Structured development programs, clear career paths, and regular feedback increase motivation and reduce turnover.
- **Leadership Development:** Succession planning and leadership training ensure a pipeline of capable leaders, safeguarding the business against tast critical role vacancies.
- **Increased Productivity:** Employees whose skills align with organizational needs perform at higher levels, driving overall business success.

- **Agility and Innovation:** A diverse, well-managed workforce is better equipped to respond to market changes and champion innovation.

To realize these benefits, organizations should invest in the following:

- Comprehensive workforce planning aligned with business strategy.
- Data-driven recruitment and selection processes.
- Continuous learning and professional development programs.
- Performance management systems that reward achievement and growth.
- Succession planning for key roles.

Additionally, leveraging technology such as HR analytics and talent management platforms can streamline processes and provide actionable insights.

Investing in talent management yields a measurable ROI through cost savings by lowering turnover rates, increasing employee engagement that leads to higher productivity and improving retention rates. The transportation and logistics company we worked with is a $50 million company. After making our recommended changes, they enjoyed higher revenue and profitability and lower employee turnover, saving the company fifty thousand dollars per employee within the first six months of employment. The estimated return on investment for the company was between $500,000 to $1 million annually. Those savings will occur annually since processes were built and implemented.

Talent management is essentially about finding the right people and placing them in the right seats or positions or "finding the right people and putting them in the right seats on the bus," as Jim Collins wrote in his book *Good to Great*. His ideas were further refined by Gino Wickman in *Traction*.

Once you have the right people in the right positions, you need to nurture or develop their abilities and keep them motivated and challenged to stay with the company. The entire talent management journey for an employee can be three years or thirty years. As we discussed, the average tenure of an employee is about 3.5 years. That tenure can vary tremendously depending on many factors. Having a well-defined and robust talent management process will greatly increase an employee's tenure. In chapter 3, we showed the financial impact of lowering your turnover rate and increasing your employee retention rate.

It may sound simple laid out like this, but the challenge is in the execution, especially in SMBs. In larger companies, where I spent much of my career, HR professionals focus solely on doing talent management for the company or certain business units in the company. SMBs don't have the luxury of hiring a person or department to do this. Usually, several people from operations fulfill this role in their spare time.

Key aspects of the talent management process include:

- **Talent acquisition** is recruiting and hiring qualified candidates. We have already discussed this in chapter 3. The key point here is that you need to have a defined, documented, and consistent process around hiring employees. Even when you do everything well, you will not be 100 percent successful in hiring. A few bad hires will slip through the recruiting process. In that case, you address them quickly and coach them up or out of the company. When you have a poor performer, you need to address the issue directly with the employee and see if they can rise to the expected performance level needed.

- **Employee development** involves training, mentorship, and opportunities for career advancement. It is a critical component in the talent management process. Understanding how an employee wants to grow in their career and what their short-term and long-term goals are critical to support their overall development, growth, and retention. If the employee has the correct skills and will to grow professionally, it is incumbent on a company to provide them with the support to make that happen. Much of this is dependent on the employee, but there must be opportunities in the company to create the path for growth simultaneously.
- **Performance management** includes evaluating employee performance and providing feedback on a continuous basis. Remember that the process itself is ongoing; it doesn't focus on the performance review itself on an annual or quarterly basis.

Talent management includes the entire employee experience with the company. In the case of employees who spend ten plus years with an employer, that journey can involve numerous critical areas of talent management. A key here for all employees is that you need to be intentional on that employee experience. Talk to your employees often about their careers and where they want to go next. By understanding the employee's career expectations over the next several years, you can better help them have the employment journey they truly want. In my corporate career there were a few times where my career desire didn't match what the company wanted me to do. In a few cases, I decided to exit that company for that exact reason. In the next chapter, we'll dive into performance management in more detail.

Chapter Six

Performance Management

The company was a $500 million business with around five hundred employees. They experienced stagnant growth and increased employee turnover over a two-year period. We worked with the leadership team to identify several challenges: unclear performance expectations, infrequent employee feedback, and lack of structured employee development opportunities. These issues resulted in inconsistent performance, low morale, and difficulty retaining top talent.

In early 2023, the company launched a comprehensive performance management initiative. The process was designed around the following key components:

- **Clear Goal Setting:** Each employee collaborated with their manager to set SMART (Specific, Measurable, Achievable, Relevant, Time-bound) goals aligned with organizational objectives that came from the executive team in January.

- **Regular Feedback and Coaching:** Managers conducted monthly one-on-one meetings to provide timely feedback, recognize achievements, and address challenges.
- **Continuous Development:** Employees were encouraged to create personal development plans as part of the monthly one-on-ones and semi-annual reviews, supported by training and mentorship programs.
- **Objective Performance Reviews:** Semi-annual reviews provided standardized criteria and peer feedback to ensure fair and transparent evaluations.

Within one year of implementing the new performance management process, the company observed significant improvements across multiple dimensions:

- **Increased Productivity:** Clearly defined goals and regular feedback helped employees prioritize their work and focus on high-impact activities. Productivity metrics, such as project completion rates and client delivery timelines, improved by 12–20 percent depending on the business line.
- **Enhanced Employee Engagement:** Annual engagement surveys showed a 25 percent increase in positive responses regarding recognition, communication, and career growth opportunities. Employees reported feeling more valued and motivated.
- **Reduced Turnover:** Voluntary turnover dropped from 22 percent to 12 percent in the year following the initiative, saving the company significant costs

associated with recruitment, onboarding and new hire training.

- **Improved Manager-Employee Relationships:** Regular one-on-one meetings fostered trust and open communication, allowing managers to address concerns early and support employee well-being.
- **Stronger Organizational Alignment:** Aligning individual goals with business objectives ensured that every employee understood their contribution to the company's mission, leading to better teamwork and effective execution of strategic initiatives.

The company experience highlights several best practices for effective performance management:

- Engage employees in their own goal setting to enhance ownership and accountability.
- Provide frequent, constructive feedback to facilitate continuous improvement. Employees often work in a vacuum with little or no feedback from their manager.
- Support ongoing learning and career development to retain top talent. Employees, especially Gen Zers and millennials, want to grow so make sure you create processes that fosters development.
- Ensure transparency and fairness in performance evaluations.
- Empower managers with training to conduct meaningful performance evaluation conversations. Most managers do not know how to do this effectively, especially with employees who are underperforming.

The performance management process is a continuous process with no real start and end point because it is cyclical in nature. By helping this client improve the entire process, the overall impact was significant. Both revenue and profitability grew, demonstrating a much healthier company than it was a few years prior.

Many people think performance management refers to a performance review or an annual review, but that's only part of it. The performance management process (PMP) is an umbrella process that includes a set of steps to grow and develop employees to support the strategic objectives of the organization. Think of the PMP as a circle without a distinct beginning or end because employees join the organization at different times of the year.

An effective performance management program will include continuous feedback, regular one-on-one conversations, coaching, goal setting, clear expectations, and a career growth plan to optimize an individual's performance. Together, they comprise performance management. To be effective, performance management is exercised throughout the year.

A performance management process works to meet company goals while channeling and optimizing employee's skills and making sure that everyone is rowing the boat in the same direction. A major benefit of performance management is employee retention. It provides an avenue for communication, feedback and accountability.

Performance management benefits include:

- Increased retention
- Improved employee engagement
- Greater productivity

- Clear performance expectations
- Higher accountability
- Aligned individual goals
- Constructive feedback
- Employee growth and development

Rowing in the Same Direction

Employees cannot meet performance expectations and company goals if they are not clearly outlined and made known. Sometimes managers are not as clear as they could be when outlining overall company goals and objectives. This is especially true the further down in the organization the manager is. The message should be repeated often so that it is top of mind to everyone, from the CEO or president to the first-line supervisor or team lead. It is beneficial to offer visuals such as wall charts, detailed PowerPoints, or emails so employees have a reference. The message should be emphasized in group and individual meetings throughout the year.

Communicate the initiative in a group meeting so everyone hears the message at the same time and no one feels singled out. It is important to tie the one-on-one meetings to your organization's core values along with emphasizing that those conversations are not meant to be a sign of dissatisfaction with an individual's work or about micromanaging. Rather, they become opportunities for getting to know each other better, learn about challenges, discuss goal setting, and to give help when needed.

Setting goals and objectives when implementing a performance management program begins by defining SMART objectives for each employee, team, and department. SMART objectives are as follows:

- **S**pecific – Make sure the goal is laser focused in nature.
- **M**easurable – Make sure you can measure the impact, time, budget and efficiency.
- **A**ttainable – Make sure the goal is achievable.
- **R**elevant – Make sure the goal is relevant to the employee's role.
- **T**ime-based – Make sure there is a time boundary, a completion date or quarter.

Many organizations set dumb goals or objectives for their employees. SMART goals are not that easy to come up with. Take the time to create SMART goals; it will pay off for you in the long run.

Creating SMART goals ensures that managers and company leaders operate from the same game plan. This makes it easier for managers and leaders to develop a set of realistic goals to measure employee progress and allows employees to set practical goals for themselves. Preparing an updated job description for your team members can also add clarity to goal setting. You can then work with your team to establish SMART goals that align with their current roles and career objectives.

One-on-One Meetings

Regular one-on-one meetings with each of your team members may sound like a burden, but meeting for fifteen to twenty minutes a month with one person adds up to no more than four to six hours over the course of a year, less than one workday annually. That's not too high a price to pay to bolster your team's and your company's performance. It also supports employee retention, prevents you from spending too much time (or not enough) recruiting and onboarding replacements, and helps each of your team members grow and achieve their goals.

Tips for the Meeting

- *Regular meetings.* Meet with each team member at least monthly for fifteen to twenty minutes. Research shows that many employees, regardless of job level, prefer frequent shorter meetings. It also correlates with the highest levels of engagement. Remember, this is not applicable during the onboarding period when meetings occur most frequently.

- *A hybrid plan* allows you to meet with some team members every two weeks. You should spend basically the same amount of time with each employee over the course of the month, regardless of which plan you choose. It may sound like a large investment of time, but leaders should be spending their time investing in their employees.

- *Team size.* If your team is ten or more, it may be best to hold individual meetings every other week to ease the schedule demands of a larger team. Frequent meetings are always better, but be realistic about what you can and cannot do.

- *Remote or in person.* If your team is remote, more frequent meetings can help counter the lack of in-person contact.
- *Employee preference.* Give your employees a voice in the decision on the cadence. Once you complete the initial twelve-week onboarding process, let the employee take part in the decision of frequency. This isn't a dictatorship; it's a partnership. Big difference.

Productive meetings depend on creating a setting in which the employee feels respected, heard and valued. That will make them more comfortable to share. Keep in mind the focus of the meeting is your employees' needs, performance, and engagement. This is *not* a project update meeting! Research shows that one of the key factors of a successful one-on-one meeting is the employee's active participation, how much they talk. Ideally, the employee would be talking 50–90 percent of the time with the manager actively listening. Managers should be careful not to talk more than the employee. If that occurs, it becomes your meeting not the employees'.

Sample Questions

- What is your favorite part of the job?
- What is your least favorite part of the job?
- Is anything slowing you down or holding you back from getting your job done right now?
- How can I help you be successful? Note that this question is critical!

- How do you rate our overall team culture on a scale of 1–10? Why did you give this numeric rating?
- What should be maintained or changed?
- Are there any particular projects, tasks, or skills that you need feedback on or help with?
- Would you like more or less coaching/direction from me?
- What would you like to be doing in one to two years from now? (If they say they would like to be in your role, don't panic. You might be in a different role by then!)
- Which part of your job most aligns with your long-term goals?

Long-Range Topics

Many times, one-on-one meetings tend to focus on immediate issues and putting out fires, but the longer-range topics like career planning and development opportunities should be woven into the meeting as well. This can be done during the last five to ten minutes of each meeting or by dedicating every third or fourth meeting to longer range topics.

End the meeting by clarifying key takeaways and action items for both parties. Define the next steps. This builds continuity between meetings and encourages follow-up. Remember that the meetings represent an evolving story which will be nurtured and developed over time. Ideally, both parties will leave the conversation feeling valued and well informed with clarity about next steps on projects, solutions to problems and the commitments that each of them has made.

Performance Differentiation

Differentiating performance is a key part of a good performance management program. Identifying your high and low performers helps improve performance by being able to celebrate the high performers and provide coaching opportunities for low performers, so they can become better at their jobs or exit the organization. It's very important that you deal with low performers early. Thousands of managers have told me they wish they had acted sooner rather than later on low performers. No one likes conflict and managers prefer not to deal with tough conversations, especially regarding performance. A key is to make sure you have written documentation on performance conversations.

At the same time, I've known hundreds of managers who were ready to fire an employee that day without any written documentation that verified the employee's performance issues. Managers don't like it when their HR person says "No, you cannot terminate the employee today. Go back and start documenting their performance issues in writing and make sure the written document clearly states that unless you improve your performance by X date there could be further disciplinary action up to and including termination of employment." It is critical to have in writing that the termination of an employee could be an outcome of the process.

Don't think that you are helping the team by avoiding dealing with low performers. This approach does not help individuals or the team. Performance differentiation is about rewarding the hard work of top performers and motivating the low performers to improve their performance. Not differentiating employee's performance will frustrate the employees and drive down overall performance. Your high performers may get so frustrated with you that they decide to look for another job because they are tired of carrying the low performers on their backs.

Managing Your Top Talent

Managing your top talent or high performers well is very challenging. Make sure you provide opportunities and support their career growth. Balance autonomy with guidance, coaching and support. Acknowledgement and appreciation are relatively low-cost ways to reinforce positive behavior and support retention. Give direct, actionable feedback to your top talent.

Ensure alignment and support motivation by sharing organizational context, vision and strategy, soliciting input where possible. Your top performers are a small percentage (typically 10–20 percent) of your employee base; they are your rock stars. Yes, this is a small percentage, but that's why you need to do everything you can to retain them. Top performers are the most cherished employees in a company. Nurture them, grow them, and protect them from being poached by a competitor. Pay them very well and challenge them with new and different work and stretch assignments that will push their capabilities.

Most high-potential employees leave a company because they aren't challenged, or they don't see a good career path ahead of them. They don't leave because of pay, unless they are not paid well to do their job. If you are paying them in the top 75–90 percentile for their position, you should be okay. Make sure you benchmark your internal pay against the external market rate at least every two years. If you don't do this, you may start losing employees because they aren't paid competitively. Make sure you stay ahead of this curve. Don't fall behind here because it's tough to make up the difference if your internal pay falls too far behind market pay.

On the other end of the spectrum, let's discuss your lower performing employees.

Managing Low Performers

Every company employs low performing employees; probably 5-10 percent of your workforce fall in this category. It is important for you to help your low performers improve their performance. Attempt to coach them *up* before showing them *out*. Letting employees go is the last option, but that does happen in many cases unfortunately.

First off, identify what is going wrong. Is it a skill or will issue or a trajectory of growth issue, or all the above? Develop an approach based on the root cause of the issue. There should be no surprises for the employee in the process. Give early and specific feedback so the individuals have enough time to fix their problems. Do not wait until the quarterly or annual review to tell an employee that something is not going well. That would be way too late and a disservice to the employee, yourself, and the company. Use your regular one-on-one meetings to signal that an issue is occurring; that's why these meetings are so important. If I had a nickel for every leader who told me they wish they had moved quicker on this performance issue and termination, I would be able to retire.

If performance coaching doesn't work, move to the disciplinary action process as outlined below. Remember, if you terminate an employee for performance reasons, this should *not* be a surprise to them. If it is, you did not do your job in giving them feedback and trying to help them work through their performance issues.

The process for managing low performers should be a standard four-step disciplinary process:

1. **Coaching conversation:** Openly discuss the issue with the employee during a one-on-one session.

2. **Verbal warning:** Talk to the employee, giving them specifics on the performance issue and setting clear expectations on what good performance looks like. Even though this is a verbal warning, email the employee to confirm that the discussion took place and copy yourself.

3. **Written warning:** Send the employee a letter, referencing the prior conversations. Make sure the warning letter explains the performance issues already discussed and what good performance looks like. The letter should also clearly state that if the performance issue does not improve, *"this could end up with further disciplinary actions up to and including termination of employment."* This statement is critical. In too many cases, an employee never knows that they could be terminated if things don't improve. Why? Because the manager never communicated it to the employee in writing. Lastly, make sure the employee signs and dates the warning letter. That way they can't claim they were never informed about the issue and what could occur.

4. **Final warning:** The last step in the process is the final warning or performance improvement plan (PIP). The process from coaching to the final warning depends on many factors. The entire process could follow a two-month and up to a six-month timeline. As I explained in step 3, refer to the prior steps and clearly state that at this point improvement must occur or termination would be an outcome.

Keep in mind this process varies slightly depending on the state in which the employee is based or other factors such as a union or non-union environment. Also, there are certain infractions that are so serious that an employee may be terminated immediately. A few examples would be falsifying timesheets, bullying of a coworker, or becoming violent in the workplace. Yes, these situations do happen in today's workplace. These strategies are essential if you want to have an effective performance management program that can work wonders when embedded into your company's culture. Consistent feedback and communication lead to higher engagement for managers and employees alike, while creating alignment of goals at all levels of the organization. Companies who have a focused performance management program are equipped to meet goals, grow revenue, and most importantly increase profitability.

Chapter Seven

Leadership Development

One of our clients, a national brand in building products in the residential and commercial building industry, worked with an outside vendor to implement a formalized process for reviewing core business processes including people. As part of the review, they identified a clear need for leadership training. The client then reached out to me to build and facilitate a yearlong leadership training program for them. Leadership development is no longer a luxury; it is a strategic imperative for organizations seeking sustainable growth, resilience, and competitive advantage.

Strong leadership is the cornerstone of any successful organization, especially Fortune 500 companies. Leaders set direction, inspire teams, navigate change, and foster innovation. Without effective leadership, organizations risk stagnation, high turnover, and missed opportunities. The leadership program we helped create included sixty to ninety minute modules to produce the building blocks that all leaders need to be effective.

The financial impact of leadership development is substantial. According to industry studies such as Society of HR Management (SHRM) article in July 10, 2025, companies that invest in leadership development see a median return of more than five times their investment.[1] The many benefits of strong leadership include improved employee performance, reduced turnover, and increased innovation, all which directly contribute to the bottom line. Additionally, intangible benefits, such as enhanced reputation and organizational agility, further strengthen the business case.

When the building company finished its first leadership development program in late 2025, the impact of the program had not been fully realized. But the initial impact and feedback was positive. The tools and techniques taught in the program have equipped these leaders to better handle the daily interactions with employees. The company plans to offer the program annually and work with me to design a program for mid-level managers.

Most middle-market companies, those with less than $500 million in annual revenue, conduct little or no training for their first-line managers or leaders—those who supervise non-managerial employees. Those leaders are typically promoted because they are good at their jobs; the criteria for promotion has nothing to do with their competency, capacity, or ability to lead people effectively.

When you think about this, it makes absolutely no sense. It's like allowing a sixteen-year-old to start driving a car simply because they have seen their mom or dad drive for years. So why not give them the car keys and tell them to have fun? Ideally, the young teen is taught how to drive a car in a safe environment, takes lessons from a parent or formal driving instructor, and learns the myriad of rules and regulations on how to drive a vehicle safely. That is what should occur with new leaders when they are promoted or better yet before they are promoted or even offered a position to lead others.

The exact same reason applies for the case to train your first-line leaders to become good leaders. Keep in mind, leaders and managers are two very different roles. Managers manage budgets, projects, timelines, quality and so on. Leaders lead people, motivate them, listen to them, delegate to them, discipline them, show them empathy, reward them, coach them, and cast a vision of the future for the company. This is a small list of what a leader should do. For more information on leadership see the references page at the end of the book.

Going back to the case for leadership, your first-line leaders are the glue or the backbone that keeps your workforce moving in the right direction. Most of your employees do not have a close connection with your executive leaders, especially in companies with over one hundred employees. Most of your employees have a much closer connection to their direct boss. That person will directly influence an employee's decision to stay at a company. They will also directly influence an employee's level of engagement. Currently, according to Gallup, the level of overall employee engagement is 31 percent, yes, 31 percent. Those employees give discretionary effort and are willing to give 110 percent or more each day. The 31 percent number has steadily gone down from a high of 36 percent in 2020. Of course, this number is a national average. Your specific employee engagement scores might be higher. If so, congratulations!

Some CEOs, business owners and private equity firms may think that they can't afford to offer training to their leaders because it's too expensive. That is a huge mistake. Yes, there is an expense to training your leaders, but it is an investment and one with a great return. You don't need to send your first-line leaders to Harvard for an MBA. That might make sense for a few high-potential, mid-level leaders in your company, but for most leaders, they need just the basic foundational tools to lead their people on a daily, weekly, and monthly basis.

Giving your first-line leaders a core set of leadership tools to add to their toolbox makes sense. Below is a list of the top six leadership traits or competencies (out of hundreds) that you should strongly consider fostering within your business as a way to get started. And it would be good to identify some of these traits in the people you plan on promoting into a supervisory or management role before promoting them.

1. Good Listener

In today's busy world, our minds race at a hundred miles per hour for eight, ten, or twelve-plus hours per day. Depending on your job, you may be in one hundred conversations (text and emails) daily. Some of these are short and others go back and forth many times.

In my years in HR, I have observed a handful of common traits in the truly great leaders. One of these traits is the art of listening. You may think listening is simply the act of not talking, but that is far from the truth. Especially if you are in a meeting with ten other people discussing a complex problem. The best leaders are those who speak the least and are great at gathering and synthesizing information.

The art of listening includes distilling information and then repeating an abbreviated version back to the other participants in many cases. You also need to determine the validity of the information being shared. Some information is highly valid, and sometimes a person is just looking for airtime and saying nothing material along the way. We all know what that looks like.

The best listeners ask great questions that really cut to the heart of the situation. They can also use silence effectively. The best salespeople can usually use silence very strategically. Americans generally don't like silence. It's like dead air on the radio; it makes us feel uncomfortable.

To become a great listener, well, you need to listen more than you are talking. For example, when you interview someone, you should be doing 20 percent of the talking and 80 percent of the listening.

Prepare a set of effective questions to draw people out, such as:

- That's fascinating, can you talk more about that?
- I'm not sure I understood that, can you restate the key points again?
- Can you describe that more clearly?
- Would you give me a specific example of what you mean?
- What do you think we should do?

Lastly, practice active listening. Active listening is when you paraphrase what the speaker said back to them during the conversation. It may sound simple, but it takes practice to perfect this skill. This is more effective in one-on-one conversations vs. group settings. It looks like this:

- Let me tell you what I heard you say.
- Let me make sure I heard you correctly.
- To recap, here's what I heard.

Good listeners make it look easy. Unless you intentionally practice it, you won't get better. Focus on a few ideas shared above and really focus on being silent as part of being a great listener.

2. Humility

Our next leadership trait is humility. To be humble is to have a modest opinion or estimate of one's own importance or rank. In today's "all about me" world it has become harder to find people who project true humility. In working with thousands of leaders over the past three decades, I have learned that truly great leaders are humble. In many cases, humility separates good leaders from great leaders.

Humility enables leaders to recognize real limits and accept others as their equal or even their superior in any given situation. Humility is needed to lead because it helps us to trust others to do the work they are tasked to do. Without humility, leaders become skeptical of others, even control freaks, and are convinced that they know better than everybody else.

To be humble is to be centered in reality. It is quite simple. It is recognizing and accepting your limitations and being self-aware about them. Humble leaders grasp their own strengths and weaknesses. It's like looking in the mirror. We sometimes don't want to see the real picture and maybe prefer to remember what our twenty-something self looked like. Truly great leaders surround themselves with leaders who are smarter than they are and think differently than they do. The same basic tenet applies today: hire smart people who think differently than you and listen to them.

Sometimes we are able to truly understand things by defining their opposites. Pride is the opposite of humility and is defined as an exaggerated self-esteem, conceit or estimate of one's own excellence. Humility is opposed by two forms of pride on a spectrum of self-centeredness ranging from extreme overconfidence to exaggerated lowliness (false humility). When you think about a sport like the NFL, we have a perfect example of humility. Many of the greatest players such as Roger Staubach or Mike Singletary were not focused on themselves; they were focused on the team. In comparison, you see many of today's players who only want to focus on how great they are and how much the team needs them.

Abraham Lincoln is a great example of humility. It has been told that a young man, consumed in his own thoughts while leaving a hospital, barreled right over Abe Lincoln. Rather than apologize, the young man yelled, "Watch where you're going, you long-legged fool!"

"What is troubling you, young man?" Lincoln asked.

He had been wronged, but his humility enabled him to accept the bigger reality that the young man's troubles likely far outweighed Lincoln's minor bruises.

"True humility is not thinking less of yourself; it is thinking of yourself less," usually attributed to C. S. Lewis, this quote builds upon the Jewish moral tradition which views deliberate attempts to achieve humility as self-defeating. Dwelling too much on oneself is directly at odds with humility, which is a focus on reality and what is truly good rather than oneself.

We all know people in our lives who control the conversation by only talking about themselves and never ask how the other person is doing. The conversation usually ends by them saying "great talking to you" without them learning anything about who or how you are.

Humility Is Open-Mindedness to the Truth

Humility cannot occur without accepting deserved criticism and compliments. A fundamental indicator of a lack of humility is an inability, even anger, toward receiving criticism from others. Years ago, a CEO gave me constructive feedback. He told me this was the gift of feedback. I could throw it away, regift it, or take it in the spirit it was given to make me better. I'll always remember his words, and I occasionally repeat them now. That CEO was a great leader. Feedback, in most cases, is given for the purpose of making you better.

I truly enjoy watching great leaders in meetings. Many times, it's very hard to determine who the leader is because they listen and ask great questions. In many cases, they don't weigh in with their opinion until they need to or if there is no decision or consensus between the other leaders in the room. Remember that humility is a great leadership trait and a mindset that is important when leading others.

3. Accountable

Accountability is an acceptance of responsibility for honest and ethical conduct toward others. In the corporate world, a company's accountability extends to its shareholders (if you have them), owners, supervisors, managers, employees, and the wider community in which it operates and serves.

In the same way, leaders need to hold themselves accountable. Accountability must go both ways or else it simply doesn't work. You need to walk the talk of accountability. In Kim Scott's book *Radical Candor*, she focuses on the importance of personally caring about employees and challenging them directly, which is a form of accountability. It's infuriating when you see leaders wanting to hold everyone else accountable except themselves. Many leaders set a double standard whereby they set rules for their teams, but the same rules do not apply to them. That's very frustrating for their employees. Bottom line, they aren't very good leaders.

The best way to create a culture of accountability is to set solid, SMART goals for every employee. Most companies, however, do not set SMART goals for their employees. Their goals are quite dumb because they are not measurable, they are not specific, have no time boundaries. Creating SMART goals is hard, which is why most leaders and employees avoid them. Once you do make the effort to create SMART goals, it can radically change your company.

If each employee, including all levels of leadership (CEO, president, GM) had SMART goals, the bar of accountability would be significantly raised throughout the company. Goal-setting should occur in the fourth quarter each year with only a small set of goals for each employee. I once worked for a Fortune 500 employer where the CEO set three goals for himself going into the next financial year. At the town hall introducing his next year's goals, he informed employees, "I run the company. If I have three goals, guess what, you can too!" In some cases, it's not realistic, but in many cases it is. Spending several hours creating SMART goals for yourself and your team can be a game changer organization wide.

The other key to accountability is to meet with employees often. I recommend short meetings with employees at least monthly to touch base. If run correctly, the meeting can be fifteen to twenty minutes. We touched on this in chapter 6. By holding these meetings monthly, you show you care for the employees by listening to them and seeing if they need your help with anything they are working on. That's what accountability looks like.

Creating a culture of accountability not only helps your business perform better, but it also sets clear expectations regarding employee performance. Most employees want to have a clear picture of where they are on performance expectations. Setting SMART goals and creating the forum for accountability is the best way to create a company culture that values setting and meeting goals and being held accountable to do so.

In the last ten to fifteen years, the role of the leader has changed tremendously. The leaders of today must look at their employees as the heart and soul of the organization. Gen Zers and millennials continue to become the largest percentage of the workforce. They are looking for a more humane, caring, and empathic company culture than baby boomers who now make up less than 20 percent of the workforce.

With the changing workforce demographics, empathy is becoming a more crucial leadership trait than it was just five years ago. Let's discuss the trait of empathy and why it's such a critical leadership trait today.

4. Empathetic

Empathy in leadership means the following:

- **Having perspective.** Having perspective means walking a mile in another person's shoes. You need to understand where they are coming from before taking any further steps or moving the conversation any further. In many situations, disagreements or arguments can be avoided if you do this first.

- **Withholding judgement.** This means not being too hasty when judging someone. You need to listen effectively and ask probing questions to gain the right information. Everyone has a level of bias, sometimes positive, other times negative. As a leader, do not judge people too quickly; that's where being a good listener comes into play.

- **Recognizing others' emotions.** An empathetic leader understands that if another person is truly frustrated or angry, it will be difficult to rationalize with them at that moment. Over the years, I have learned that many times employees just want a safe place to vent. They don't want advice, coaching, or an opinion. Oftentimes, an upset employee would come into my office, vent for thirty minutes and say thank you afterward. At first, I was honestly confused because I would ask myself why are they thanking me. About ten years later I realized that all I needed to do in this situation was listen and occasionally nod my head. They didn't want an answer or solution; they simply wanted to be heard.

- In today's world, we naturally go into problem-solving mode. If you're a parent, you fully understand this point. Remember, in many cases, listening and showing empathy for the person is all that's needed.
- **Listening for understanding.** Listening effectively to truly gain understanding is an art form. Salespeople, interviewers, and every leader needs to be able to listen for understanding, not just listen for the sake of listening.
- In today's changing workforce, employees want very different things from employers than they did in the 1990s and early 2000s. Gone are the days of unwavering employee loyalty. Loyalty still exists, but on a different level. Today, employees want a great culture, a strong purpose in the company's mission, and to work with leaders who want to know the employee as a person. The best companies are those that love, care for, and show empathy to their employees. These are companies that experience less difficulty in hiring employees. In most cases, they are also the companies that perform better financially compared to their competition.

5. Self-Aware

Self-awareness is a critical leadership trait that enables individuals to recognize their strengths, weaknesses, and emotional responses. Effective leaders are not only better attuned to their own behaviors and motivations, but they also appreciate how their actions impact others.

This awareness fosters honest self-reflection, which leads to better decision-making and authentic relationships within teams. Self-aware leaders are open to feedback and willing to adapt, creating a culture of trust and continuous improvement. By understanding themselves, self-aware leaders can more effectively guide, inspire and support those around them, ultimately driving organizational success. In best-case scenarios, leaders with high self-awareness focus on bringing employees onto their team who think and/or act differently than they do to make the team stronger.

The first five traits are being a good listener, humble, accountable, empathetic, and self-aware. Of course, hundreds of other leadership traits exist as well. These are the five that I have found are the X factor for many good leaders I have worked with in my professional career.

6. Visionary

The last trait to round out the top six list is being a visionary. It is probably the most challenging for most leaders. In my career, I can count the true visionary leaders I have worked for on two hands with room to spare.

The visionary *ponders and plans the future with imagination or wisdom*. It sounds so simple, but it is so hard to accomplish. Why? In most cases, the fire of the day or week gets in the way of most CEO/Presidents, owners, and executives, especially in middle-market companies where leaders often wear many hats. At HR Catalyst, we primarily work with companies with fewer than 250 employees. In most cases, the CEO/President still drops into tactical mode and gets in the middle of firefighting weekly.

I'm a realist here and for most middle-market companies, the CEO/President/Owner can be visionary or strategically focused at most about 50 percent of the time on a good month or year. This is true because they likely work with a leadership team composed of A, B, and in some cases C players. This is especially true in fast-growing companies where many leaders were A players five years ago. Unfortunately, as the business grows and becomes more complex, the capacity to operate as an A player may no longer exist because the role is bigger than the person's capacity or competence level to perform the job. They have hit a ceiling and can't perform any higher. Many leaders can perform successfully when the company was $10 million in revenue, but when the company is $30 or $50 million in revenue or larger, certain leaders may no longer be able to perform well and in some cases may slow the company down.

A great example of this is the number of players who play college football and then go on to play in the NFL. About 1.6 percent move from college to pro ranks. In addition, many NFL players may never play in a game. They play on the practice squad and get the team ready for their next game. Most companies don't have the luxury of having A players in all key leadership roles. The other key reason is that the top role in the company is led by an incumbent who is truly more operational than strategic in focus. Only about 1 in 10,000 leaders are truly visionary. Think of Martin Luther King Jr., Nelson Mandela, Steve Jobs, Winston Churchill, Leonardo Davinci, and Mother Teresa for example. That is a very elite group of leaders.

For us mere mortals, the following paragraph describes some things we can do to become more strategic or visionary in our focus.

Focus on the external versus internal factors that impact your company. Take a look at what is going on outside your company - macroeconomics, political influences, industry trends, supply chain issues all of which can strongly impact your business. The more you focus outside your business the better. Attend conferences, join a professional organization in your city or peer advisory groups like Vistage, Convene, or C12, for example. Be intentional about continuing to develop your career. If you aren't learning something new each year, you are going backward.

Conduct a one or two day strategic planning session at least annually with your business leaders. Bring in an external facilitator to conduct the session and challenge the status quo within your organization. Ask questions like "why do we do this?" and "what if we did that?" in your strategic planning sessions. Even better, ask employees what's broken or needs improvement in your organization. If you ask employees these questions, you may be amazed with the answers you get back. In many cases, employees know what's broken, the leaders or owners don't, because they are too far removed from the day to day operations. Some leaders may respond by saying, "The way we do it now has always worked." If you hear that, be worried, be very worried that your leadership team has become too complacent.

If you are on the executive leadership team within your business, challenge yourself to spend 30–50 percent of your time working *on* your business rather than *in* your business. What does this look like? Determine the latest trends in your business. What are your toughest competitors doing that your company isn't? Talk to your top ten customers at least annually and ask them what you can do better or what you can improve. Even better, talk to customers who fire you and ask them why they did that. The more time you spend as a leader focused on external factors the better. You are paid to be looking six, twelve, twenty-four months into the future, not looking backward in your business. If you aren't doing that now, I challenge you to start doing that in the fourth quarter of your financial year. That's a great time to conduct a strategic planning session to focus on the future.

Remember that one of the top three reasons employees leave a company is they do not trust or respect their direct manager. Of course, many other factors are at play here, but a company has control over whether they train their leaders or not. Companies that don't train their leaders are at high risk for high turnover, lack of employee engagement, falling short of company goals or KPIs, and missing out on good-performing or high-performing teams.

The worst-case scenario is when an untrained leader creates a major liability risk for a company by allowing unprofessional conduct within their team or being a party to unprofessional or possibly illegal activities. In some instances, the leader should know better, but in other cases, they simply don't know what they don't know. In those cases, the company has no one else to blame but themselves. In that case the executive leadership or ownership would be the culprit.

I have witnessed too many situations where a leader in the company innocently did something that ended up in legal action against the company. In several of those cases, the legal fees alone went well into the hundreds of thousands of dollars.

That is the hard cost of an employee lawsuit. The soft cost (all of the time, effort, and overall executive distraction and worry) is something that can't be calculated but will often exceed the hard cost of a litigation, depending on how long the litigation takes.

I believe all of this should paint a compelling case for equipping your leaders with a baseline level of leadership training. You owe it to the company and your employees to equip your leaders with the tools to be successful. You wouldn't throw your car keys over to your sixteen year old without any training, would you? Don't do that to your newly promoted leader either. Give them the tools and training to add to their toolkits to be successful. They deserve that and your employees deserve that too.

Chapter Eight

Succession Planning

Succession planning is a strategic process that ensures leadership continuity and organizational stability by proactively identifying and developing internal talent to fill key positions. In today's rapidly changing business environment, the value of effective succession planning cannot be overstated. It is a critical factor for long term success, risk mitigation, and competitive advantage.

The owner of a construction business was in his late fifties and was thinking about either selling the company or looking for a successor who would like to eventually take over the company. He had never formally conducted a succession planning process and didn't really know where to start.

For over three years I worked with him to build a successor pipeline. One individual clearly showed the leadership capability and interest in taking over the business from a financial perspective. During that time, the owner continued to step out of the day-to-day operations of the business and changed his focus to business development and strategic partnerships.

The transition period continued for several more years, whereby the appointed successor gradually took more and more of an ownership stake in the business to the point that he became the majority owner of the business. The founder finally did retire about six years after the succession planning process began. The new owner continued to grow the business and the founder was able to start the next chapter of his life.

Succession planning is not merely a human resources exercise but a business imperative. It ensures leadership continuity, enhances employee engagement, and equips organizations to thrive in the face of change. By prioritizing succession planning, companies can safeguard their future, drive sustainable growth, and maintain a competitive edge.

Succession planning is a critical business process first and foremost that looks at your talent pool especially at the executive level of your organization. In most US organizations today, the leadership team is composed of baby boomers (born 1946–1964), and Gen Xers (born 1965–1980). Many younger boomers and most Gen Xers are still working and often hold senior level positions throughout companies.

Succession planning is needed for two key reasons:

1. Identifying successors for your handful of key leadership positions. You need to identify successors, plural, since many mishaps can happen to your successor pool, such as exit from the business, retirement, major health issue, or possibly death.

2. Identifying your high potentials (hi-pos), the next generation of leaders who are ideally in their 30's and 40's. They have a long career runway and need to be identified, developed, and retained. One of the

top reasons why hi-pos leave a company is because they feel their career growth has stagnated or they hit a brick wall. They see no growth and development where they are and they feel unchallenged. They get bored and decide to dust off their resumes and leave the company. Thoroughbred employees get bored quickly so keep them challenged and engaged so you can retain them in your business.

The process of succession planning in business is very similar to any professional sports team. Every NFL team has multiple people for each position. Every team has a starting quarterback. Then they have at least a second and third string quarterback. If the starter gets hurt, they immediately know who the backup is. The backup quarterback practices with the starting offense, taking snaps in practice with them throughout the week.

Every NFL team drafts new players in April each year from the college ranks. Each team spends thousands of hours reviewing and assessing who they should draft based on many factors. In business, you hire new employees throughout the year. Like a football team, you need to spend a great deal of time in your selection and recruitment process. I discuss this in chapter 3.

Even if you have a younger executive team, you need to conduct succession planning for your business. As mentioned before, changes can happen within the executive team at any point and time. Someone could resign, be terminated, poached by a recruiter, or could experience a major health event.

When I worked for Texas Instruments years ago, the CEO at the time, Jerry Junkins, was in his mid-fifties. He was a runner, but he died unexpectedly while on a business trip. Fortunately, the company had been doing succession planning work for years and seamlessly moved one of his successors into the CEO position to continue moving the business forward.

How often should you conduct a succession planning session? I highly recommend doing this annually. We help many of our longer term clients do this. Once a year is a good starting point since businesses change constantly. If your business is growing rapidly, experiencing changes in your executive team, or is acquiring companies as part of your growth plan, you may need to conduct the succession planning sessions more often.

How do I start the process? The key thing here is to *start the process*. Any company with more than thirty employees should conduct a succession planning meeting every year. The process may only take two to four hours to complete. The key is to talk about your top leadership talent and discuss your high potential employees. If a key leader is planning to retire in twelve months, you need to develop a transition plan. If you have a key leader who is not performing well, you need to devise a coaching plan for them or exit strategy if the performance issues have been prolonged and coaching and discipline have been unsuccessful.

The process can be simple. Look at your organization chart for your executive or leadership team and list the possible successor(s). Ideally, successors are several employees not just one individual. In smaller companies, those with fewer than one hundred employees, for example, there may be several positions with no immediate successor waiting in the wings. Don't panic; it's okay. The key is to list *possible* successors and their readiness to take on the next level role. Readiness, as it sounds, depends on how long the person would take to be considered ready for the role.

Readiness should be categorized in increments of 0-12 months, 12-24 months, and 24+ months. The key exercise around readiness is to carefully think through the possible successors for the key role and then determine the employee's readiness to take on the role. This accomplishes two things for your business:

1. It identifies the logical successors for different roles.
2. It determines what a career development plan looks like for successors.

Being able to identify career development plans or individual development plans is critical for all employees, but extremely critical for employees in the succession plan. The process also applies to hi-pos, that next generation of leaders who may take on key leadership roles in the future.

When considering the succession planning process, think about differences between the games of chess and checkers. Compared to chess, checkers is quite simple. Chess is highly strategic while checkers is much more tactical. A master chess player may be planning five or more moves ahead. Similarly, succession planning is strategic in nature since the process will continue to evolve due to many dynamics in the leadership team and where the organization is going each month, quarter, and year.

Another great output of the succession planning process is to identify strategic gaps in your leadership team. If you have a key leader, let's say your VP of operations, who is retiring in nine months and no successors are ready to assume that role, you may need to go into the external market and hire a replacement. You might be able to figure that out without doing succession planning, but the process reveals the risk and also gives it the sense of urgency it deserves. You probably need to engage an outside recruiting firm for executive level positions, which can take three to six months. You're better off being proactive instead of reactive.

As you consider succession planning, remember your hi-pos are your diamonds in the rough. In most cases, your hi-pos are your A players. They are not only exceptional performers, but they fit your company culture very well, almost like brand ambassadors for your culture. When you think of hi-pos, they are a small percentage of your employee population, probably 10–15 percent at the most, but their overall performance is exceptional. They not only do great work, but they can also handle complex issues that other employees can't solve.

Succession planning helps to identify those hi-pos. As your organization grows, if the CEO, president, and executive leadership don't know who the hi-pos are, they need to get to know them. In many cases a company grows, opens multiple offices, or is fully remote, making it hard to know who they are. Succession planning helps you identify your hi-pos and gets them on the radar of the executive team. So, when an executive goes to the office in Miami, let's say, that person should spend time with the hi-pos in that location. Take them out for lunch or dinner and let them know they are recognized and appreciated by the top leadership.

You want to identify and *retain* them. If you lose a hi-po, it hurts the company today, tomorrow, and next year. You are losing a current high performer *and* a possible future leader within the company. If the person leaves the company, you may have lost a half-million-dollar employee. You may think that's impossible. Here's why I'm saying this with a high degree of confidence. Forget about their current total compensation. You are losing someone who performs at an exceptional level and who will be very hard to replace. Not only that, but the time required to get that new employee to be 100 percent productive may take six to twelve months or longer. Think about the time and dollars lost during that process and that new hire may never be as good as the high potential that you lost. A Michael Jordan or Simone Biles doesn't come along very often.

As I discussed earlier, hi-pos need challenging work. They get bored easily and need stretch assignments that excite them, make them work hard and challenge them. They want to add more skills and tools into their toolbox. Doing the same job for several years will bore them to death. A hi-po who is bored is a hi-po who is a retention risk.

Ask your hi-pos what excites them or bores them in their current role. Ask them, questions like "Are you ready to take on new assignments or different types of work? If so, what would you like to do? Where would you like to be in the company in one to three years? What can I do to help you get there to achieve that goal?" That last question is a magical one. Leaders are there to lead people; managers are there to manage things like a budget. Leaders motivate, inspire, cast the vision of the company.

Remember that hi-pos need to be paid well. We do a lot of compensation benchmarking work at our company. Make sure your hi-pos are paid at the 75–90 percentile of their pay range or external compensation range. That is a given. When a headhunter mentions a compensation number that's 20, 30, 40 percent higher than what they currently make, watch out. Moderately paid hi-pos are a *huge* retention risk for you. If that same headhunter calls and mentions a salary comparable to what they are currently making, they are more likely to say, "Thanks, but I'm good where I'm at right now."

To recap, succession planning is a critical business process, especially for companies with fifty plus employees that are growing. The process is as important as selection and hiring, budget forecasting, and sales and marketing. Companies that are growing need to understand who the successors are for executive level positions and who their hi-pos are so that they can develop and retain them. This is not a nice thing to do; it's a leadership imperative. All great companies do succession planning; that's just good business.

Chapter Nine

Total Compensation

We recently worked with a growing construction company based in Dallas. They had grown significantly in the previous five years and hired many Gen Zers and millennials during that time. As the organization grew, they needed to create a more formalized approach to compensation. This business case outlines the key benefits of implementing robust compensation strategies and demonstrates how such practices contribute to the overall success of a company.

The Strategic Value of Compensation

Every executive team needs a general awareness about total compensation practices and how they encompass not only base salaries, but also bonuses, benefits, paid time off (PTO) and recognition programs. Working with this company's team, we designed an employee awareness program that informed them on the definition of total compensation to foster engagement and create a culture of fairness and transparency. We also created career ladders for the company for their core positions to show career growth and drive employee retention. The point is to move away from the mentality of holding a job to enjoying a career with room to grow, develop and ultimately make a higher salary. By creating such transparency, employees understood why they were paid what they were paid. They also clearly understood what it required to move into another role with a higher pay level. Good compensation practices become a crucial differentiator not only to retain employees, but also to attract the right talent to support the company's continued growth.

Our engagement with the client occurred over a nine month period. Once the compensation framework and system were created, recruiting metrics improved with the time to fill a position (TTF) going down by 23 percent and the employee turnover dropping from 16 percent to 11 percent over a twelve-month period. The cost impact is hard to quantify, but we estimated a cost savings of between $500,000 and $2,000,000 annually based on their current growth and employee headcount.

Employees understanding how they can progress in a company helps them work from a career mindset rather than a job mindset, which impacts retention. If a person thinks they have a job and are offered 5-10 percent more to move into another job, there is a high likelihood they will leave the company for the better paying job.

If you can change the narrative to get employees to see career progression and how they can achieve that with your company, their mindset will move to a career focus rather a job focus. A career mindset is long term, a job focus isn't. It ends up being about what I'm being paid today.

The company created a culture of employee transparency, effectively building career ladders, so everyone knew the pay ranges and how to progress from one compensation level to another. The initial feedback was very positive and appreciated by employees.

When we think of compensation, let's make sure to set the framework clearly. Total compensation is not only pay, but it also includes many other facets such as PTO or vacation, healthcare benefits, possibly company bonuses, profit sharing or other variable compensation.

This book is geared towards SMBs or lower middle-market-sized companies with fewer than five hundred employees so let's keep that in mind. We'll focus on base compensation, either hourly pay (non-exempt employees) or salaried pay (exempt employees) that is annualized. Next, pay varies depending on where your company and the employee is based. If your business is based in nine locations, make sure you are paying competitively for the local market of where the employee lives. Employees in Little Rock, Arkansas make less than those in Dallas, Texas and those in New York City, for example. Make sure you aren't overpaying in one location and underpaying in another. This is very important because many companies have employees based remotely in different US cities. The employee should be paid based on where they are actually located not where the company is located.

Next, make sure you understand pay for your various positions. You can find basic information through LinkedIn, Indeed, Salary.com or Payscale.com. At HR Catalyst we use Payscale to run very customized compensation reports for our clients on a project basis. The free information is okay, but it's free, so make sure you look at several different websites to ensure accuracy.

Next, make sure you review pay on an annualized basis for all employees. Remember that we say *review* pay. We didn't say that every employee should receive an annual increase. Some workers may have been employed for six months and are currently paid very competitively. Others may be poor performers and definitely do not deserve a pay increase. Why does it make sense to give a poor performing employee an increase? It's like giving your child an allowance for making their beds, cleaning their rooms and taking out the trash. If they do none of those, would you still give them an allowance? Nope. Why do that for your worst employees?

The pay market will continue to change constantly based on inflation and competition for employees. The labor market is shrinking and will continue to do so for the foreseeable future. Baby boomers are retiring every day and millennials and Gen Zers are not a big enough workforce to replace them. Of course, there are many other factors at play. A competitive global workforce and artificial intelligence (AI) is becoming a major factor in every company. AI is not going away so embrace it or be left behind by your competitors. It can replace very routine or standardize processes that employees currently do twenty, fifty, or a hundred times daily. You don't pay AI, it doesn't take vacations and it usually makes fewer mistakes. Every business owner needs to learn more about AI now, not later. Remember, thirty years ago people assumed the Internet was not a business tool. Nowadays, when your company's Internet goes down many businesses can't do anything until it comes back up.

Now back to pay. Making sure that you at least review employee's pay annually is a best practice. Understanding your high-performing (hi-po) employees is critical. They're your A players and need to be retained at all costs.

Most companies review employee salaries on an annual basis, typically during the January to March time frame. When you are reviewing employee pay, make sure you differentiate pay. If you set a salary increase budget of 3.5 percent, that is based off your total payroll. So, if your payroll is $10,000,000, your salary increase budget would be $350,000 for your employees. Make sure you differentiate pay increases based on employee performance. It makes no sense to give all of your employees a 3.5 percent increase. That would mean your best and worst performers would get the same increase. That's not only bad business, but it also makes no sense.

Here is a realistic example of how to use your salary increase budget wisely. If your salary increase budget is 3.5 percent, you can give a range of pay increases between 0 percent and 8 percent. Your top performers should receive a 6–8 percent increase, while your lower performers should receive a 0–2 percent increase. Reward your top performers to stay and lower their retention risk. Incent your lower performers to increase their performance or look for other jobs outside of your company. If you reward your low performers with a 3 percent salary increase, you not only upset your high performers, but you also incent your lower performers to stay and not change their behavior. You're in business to make a profit, aren't you?

The other factor in compensation is the bonus. In many cases bonus pay is reserved for your managerial team, those who have more responsibilities and make a higher salary than other employees. In other organizations, all employees are eligible for bonus pay, which is great. Bonuses should always be based on certain business metrics, such as hitting a specific revenue target and profit or net income target. Many of our clients also include personal performance metrics that are based on hitting certain KPIs or specific annual SMART goals. Bonuses are usually set annually or semi-annually with most of our clients. I don't advise quarterly bonuses. It's too much unnecessary work preparing them and then paying them.

I also recommend that you set bonuses at certain percentage of the base salary based on the position. For example, supervisors might be paid 5 percent of their salary, managers 10 percent, directors 20 percent, and VPs at 30 percent. If a director makes $100,000 base salary, then their target payout would be 20 percent or $20,000. That math will work for the other examples as shown above. If you don't already follow this method, I highly recommend moving to a set bonus structure as shown. We discussed earlier that the sooner you create consistent HR processes, the better. These are all critical for the scalability of your company.

Chapter Ten

Employee Engagement

Employee engagement refers to the emotional commitment employees feel toward their organization and its goals, resulting in motivated, proactive, and loyal team members. A client in the transportation and logistics industries that we worked with for several years was having a problem with employee engagement. One of the first tasks with the company was to survey the entire workforce with a customized employee survey that we created with the HR team. We needed to determine what the baseline level of employee engagement was before we could address anything else. We also needed to understand the problem areas so they could be addressed.

Through the engagement survey, we (the internal HR team and myself) identified the areas with lower scores, which included employee communications, rewards and recognition, leadership trust, and understanding company strategy. We then shared the results with employees as a way to promote healthy engagement. Even if there are poor results, company executives need to be transparent and share them with employees. We discussed the results and then people volunteered to be part of teams composed of employees who wanted to help address the issues. Managers and executives were not included so the teams could work without outside bias from leaders or fear of retribution.

The company has distributed the engagement survey every eighteen months since it began five years ago. The engagement scores have continually increased, starting at 38 percent in year one and rising to 53 percent at the last survey. The employee turnover rate has decreased from 19 percent to 12 percent, and revenue and profitability have both increased in the last three years. Of course, the positive financial numbers could have been due to many factors, but employee engagement would be a key reason why the top and bottom line numbers have improved.

The company continues to look for ways to improve its engagement scores since they have shown that higher employee engagement scores can drive key metrics that lead to better financial results. More engaged employees are more productive and that increased productivity leads to better financial performance and higher levels of customer satisfaction.

Employee engagement is measured in three categories: engaged, disengaged, and actively disengaged. Understanding employee engagement is critically important because disengaged, and actively disengaged employees cost companies in the U. S. between $450 - $500 billion dollars annually in lost productivity, that's a conservative figure. Employee engagement has been in decline in the United States. The current average employee engagement level is 31 percent. Unfortunately, that number has been declining every year since 2020, when the engagement rate was at 36 percent. Let's look at employee engagement more closely.

Engaged employees are focused on work, highly productive, and go above and beyond their normal job duties. If there is a big deadline for a project, an engaged employee will stay late or get to work early to make sure the deadline is met and perhaps met early. The employee enjoys their work and the people they work with and want to give their best each day. Many employees don't think this way at work.

Disengaged employees get their jobs done, nothing more, nothing less. These employees are mainly working for a paycheck and do the basics to not be put on any type of disciplinary action notice. In most companies, around 50 percent of your employees fall into this category.

Actively disengaged employees are typically your low performing employees. They cause most of your employee issues and usually cause other negative damage in the company. In many cases, it would be best if the employee worked somewhere else besides your company.

A myriad of reasons explain why an employee is disengaged or actively disengaged. It could be a motivation issue, competence issue, or they only want to do what they are told to do and need to be micromanaged all the time.

Given the basics on employee engagement, what can you do to improve engagement? You must pay attention to your employees. Conduct regular one-on-one meetings to touch base and show them that you are actually interested in them and their well-being. You need to care about all of your employees. If you do that, they will often be more engaged. Remember, if you treat employees like a number, then they'll give you the basics. If you treat them like a person and look for ways to take care of that person, there's a good chance they will look for ways to support you and the company.

Declines in Employee Engagement

Among the twelve engagement elements that Gallup measures, those that saw the most significant declines (by three points or more in *strongly agree* ratings) in 2024 include:

- **Clarity of expectations.** Just 46 percent of employees clearly know what is expected of them at work, down ten points from a high of 56 percent in March 2020.[1]
- **Feeling someone at work cares about them as a person.** Currently, 39 percent of employees feel strongly that someone cares about them, a drop from 47 percent in March 2020.
- **Someone encouraging their development.** Only 30 percent strongly agree that someone at work encourages their development, down from 36 percent in March 2020.

This shows us that employees seek role clarity, strong relationships, and opportunities for development, but managers are progressively failing to meet these basic needs. However, managers themselves are faring no better than those they manage with only 31 percent being engaged.

The Broader Economic Context

This decline in employee engagement occurred in a challenging economic environment. Job vacancies continued to surpass hiring rates, but fewer people in 2024 said it was a good time to find a job. Quit rates are trending slightly down from the 2021–22 peaks, as reported by the Bureau of Labor Statistics (BLS), but they remain near their longer-term averages.

Leaders working to strengthen their employee engagement strategy should consider three points:

- The quality of work is only one aspect of productivity and is especially difficult for the BLS to measure. The BLS typically measures productivity as the ratio of revenue to hours worked (labor productivity), which is not a measure of work quality. Output per worker can result from technological advances, the rising value of intellectual property or capital investments.
- The involvement and enthusiasm employees feel toward their work and workplace predicts numerous outcomes across business units within companies including quality of work, safety, profitability and more.
- Recent findings from The Conference Board suggest CEOs had lower confidence in their own industries in late 2024.

Employee engagement trends matter for organizational leaders because declines signal potential vulnerabilities for businesses. Broad macroeconomic indexes do not always reflect what leaders and employees are experiencing in their own workforces and industries.

The factors that affect macro conditions do not necessarily align with the micro conditions, such as the quality of leading others, that directly affect how employees feel at work every day, their individual productivity and their well-being. Moreover, macroeconomic conditions, such as unemployment rates, inflation and interest rates, can limit the success of individual organizations that have little to do with the engagement of their workforce. For instance, when mortgage rates are high, even the most engaged and skilled real estate agents struggle to close deals compared with periods with lower rates.

Gallup research attributes declining employee engagement and rising detachment to:

- *Rapid organizational change.* The pace of change continues to escalate and the long-term impact of AI on the workforce is still being determined.
- *Hybrid and remote growing pains.* Many organizations are still learning how to effectively manage remote and hybrid employees. Companies with a large percentage of these workers must make leading this workforce a priority.
- *New customer and employee expectations.* Customers continue to expect more from their vendors - what I call the "Amazon phenomena." At the same time, employees want more from the employee experience than ever before.
- *Broken performance management practices.* Companies must continually train managers how to engage in meaningful one-on-one conversations with employees who want connection and purpose at work. This effort begins with leadership and organizational culture.

Companies must also ensure employees are working toward clear SMART goals, a topic discussed earlier.

How to Improve Employee Engagement

Despite declining overall US engagement, many organizations Gallup has studied have achieved and maintained engagement levels more than twice the national average. Despite the significant challenges workplaces have faced since 2020, strong leaders and managers can reverse declining engagement by focusing on these strategies:

- *Define what employees want in their workplace culture and how that aligns with the organization's purpose and value to customers.* Be transparent in communications from the executive team on down. When times are good, celebrate them; when times are challenging, explain the situation to employees and involve them in developing solutions. Too often, I have seen companies lack transparency in communications with employees, which only creates distrust and lowers engagement.

- *Lead with your organization's strengths while clearly communicating its purpose, approach to people, key decisions, and performance expectations.* Include a plan to upskill managers so they can build stronger bonds between employees and the organization through clear priorities, ongoing feedback, and accountability.

- *Prioritize identifying and selecting managers who have the innate ability to engage and inspire employees.* This is especially important in workplaces where employees feel detached. Conduct annual succession-planning sessions to ensure strong leadership pipelines within your company.

I work with several clients with fewer than two hundred employees that do a great job in the three areas mentioned above. This is not rocket science. It goes back to understanding the employee's needs and working towards fulfilling them.

Chapter Eleven

Offboarding

We discussed employee onboarding in chapter 4. In this chapter, we will look at the offboarding process. Employees leave a company for many reasons. It could be a spousal relocation, a significantly better offer or promotional opportunity from another company, a move to care for an elderly parent, retirement, and so on. When we think about onboarding and offboarding it's good to remember the old adage, you want to make the first impression and last impression the best they can be. Of course, in some cases, an employee may be terminated by the company, which doesn't usually leave a good impression. We aren't discussing that here.

When an employee voluntarily resigns from the company, they typically will give at least two weeks' notice, a professional courtesy that is still expected. There are cases where an employee will text their boss and inform them that they quit. Unfortunately, that is becoming more prevalent in today's workforce. If that does occur, the chance of you rehiring that employee is slim to none.

If the employee gives you a two-week notice and they are working on a critical project, you might be able to extend their notice period to a month or possibly longer. Of course, that will be based on their future employer and the employee themselves. I have seen times where a good employee in this situation can stay for a longer notice period, four to six weeks in some cases.

If an employee has worked for you for several years and been a solid performer, you want to make sure they are treated well as they exit the company. About 28 percent of employees return to their former employer, hence the reason to treat the employee with respect on their departure. I tend to call that "the grass is greener" phenomena. In most situations, the grass may be a different shade of green at another company, but it's not actually greener. Every company has issues of some kind, some bigger, some smaller. There is no perfect company because companies are run by people and every person has weaknesses that cloud their judgement in some way.

With over one quarter of your employees being *returning* employees (coming back a second or even third time in some cases), make sure you treat a departing employee with the same level of professionalism and respect you treat current ones. Conduct an exit interview with them to find out specifically why they are leaving the company. In many cases, you'll discover a great deal of good information. In most cases, you want an internal HR professional to conduct the exit interview, if possible, since the reason why the person is exiting may be due to their direct boss.

The exit interview should entail a set of five to ten questions that you use consistently with each person who is leaving on good terms. Here is a sample list of questions that you can use as a starting point.

- *What prompted you to begin looking for another opportunity?* This helps identify underlying issues that may be driving turnover.
- *What factors influenced your decision to leave the organization?* HR uses this to understand whether the departure relates to compensation, management, culture, or career growth.
- *How would you describe your experience working with your manager and team?* This question can surface leadership or team dynamics that may need improvement.
- *Did you feel you had the resources, training, and support needed to perform your job effectively?* Responses help identify gaps in onboarding, training, or operational support.
- *What did you like most about working here, and what could have been improved?* This provides balanced feedback on strengths and weaknesses in the workplace.
- *What suggestions would you offer to improve the employee experience for others in this role or department?* This invites constructive recommendations that can guide organizational improvement.

Ask them, if things change, would they be interested in returning in the future. This will gauge their interest level to return even before they have formally exited. You may even want to consider a recruitment campaign for former employees. Email them every few months and tell them about job openings, exciting news about the company, and things like that. Remember the cost of hiring that we discussed in an earlier chapter? Doesn't it make sense to spend time and effort to recruit good former employees?

Some companies reach out to former employees a few times in their first six months after leaving. Remember the "grass is greener" statement I mentioned earlier. The employee may find out that the new employer or position isn't what the employer portrayed during the interview. The boss may be a jerk, or the company might be going through a restructuring, and the job they were offered may be changing significantly, or worse, it may be eliminated. If you do a simple outreach campaign to employees in the first six months after their departure, you may get a few former employees running back to you quickly. Their skills and cultural fit would still be great and there is little to no ramp up time to get them back to being fully productive in their role. For all these reasons, it makes perfect sense to recruit former employees to see if a few or more may return annually.

Chapter Twelve

Change Management

The ability to manage change effectively ensures that strategic initiatives are realized, investments yield returns, employees are retained, and competitive advantages are sustained. An Aerospace manufacturing company I consulted was going through major growth inorganically. They were acquiring companies across the country every three to four months to further increase their capability, capacity and national footprint. With the aggressive growth came the need for a strong change management process. Without an effective change management process, the organization would risk employee resistance, decreased morale, loss of productivity, and higher employee turnover.

My role was to identify and build a common infrastructure for core HR processes. This allowed for the smooth and speedy integration of the acquired companies. Employees knew what was occurring quickly instead of changes occurring over several months. The faster you can get back to business, the less productivity will be lost that would create revenue lost.

Over the eighteen month period that I was consulting the company I successfully completed multiple acquisitions while still maintaining a high level of employee engagement and profitability. Overall, the private equity firm that was managing the company felt like the overall growth strategy was a success and the strategic objectives were met.

When most employees hear about a change in their company, there typically have one of two emotional reactions based on your psychological makeup: excitement or fear. Half the people see a glass half full and are excited. Half the people see a glass half empty and are afraid. How a person views the situation depends on their upbringing; they are either highly optimistic or pessimistic.

In this chapter, we are going to focus on the myriad of changes that occur within a company. Companies are ever-changing ecosystems, from start-up to growth to survival to thriving.

When the COVID-19 pandemic hit in March 2020 companies needed to change quickly. Many businesses could not react fast enough and went out of business. Other businesses were able to make changes and keep their employees safe and work under the "new normal." This was highly challenging in manufacturing environments and the hospitality industry.

In most organizations, major changes impact employees in a significant way. Therefore, human resource departments must be heavily involved in supporting any change at a company. Change impacts people, and the HR department is there to support communications and lead other facets regarding the change process. I have been involved in several major companywide change programs both in my consulting days and when I was in corporate HR roles. Preparing a well thought out and comprehensive change process is critical for the success of any change.

Why is a company-wide change so challenging? It involves many people. It is not uncommon for the leadership team to disagree on why the change is needed. When that occurs, the chance for success is limited. A company needs to get alignment at the executive team level first. I said *alignment* not 100 percent *agreement*. Depending on the impact of the organizational change, not all executives may agree with the change, but they must be aligned that the change is needed to present a unified front. If not, employees will quickly figure out the lack of cohesion, and the change may be doomed to fail.

Employees perceive change differently than their leaders. Leaders look at things more long term and will see the change in a very positive way, whereas employees may see the change as being disruptive to their everyday lives. Something else that complicates change efforts is when they are not scoped correctly before it is started. Change is in jeopardy when the leaders haven't factored well the time needed, resources needed, budget needed and effort needed. Another roadblock to successful change is when company-wide communications regarding the change are poorly done. In many cases, the communications plan is the last consideration and done quickly and poorly. One of the biggest reasons changes fail is due to the lack of a good communications plan. Make sure you focus on communications as a priority not an afterthought.

In many cases, poor communications during change occurs because leaders are simply tired of working through and discussing the change. This could especially be true when doing a system or technology change or acquiring another company for a strategic reason. These changes can be very lengthy and highly complex, and the executive team wants to get back to business rather than rationalizing the change to their employees.

Top Reasons Employees Resist Change

- *Loss of Control.* When anyone loses control, they feel uncomfortable to a certain extent. If you have ever slid on an icy road while driving, you fully understand what I'm talking about. The last thing you want to do is hit the brakes. Change interferes with autonomy, and most employees want a level of autonomy. If you have ever taught a child to drive, not being in the driver's seat can be frightening, and in some cases hazardous!

- Smart leaders leave room for those affected by change to make choices. They invite lower-level managers into the planning that affects their area, giving them a sense of ownership. In many cases, they might bring key hi-po employees into the decision-making process.

- *Excess Uncertainty.* People often prefer to remain mired in misery than head toward the unknown. Leaders should cast the vision and present clear, simple steps and timetables in order to inspire confidence in the employees that the change is positive. They should explain to employees why the change is happening and what the benefits will be.

- *More Work.* Change is indeed more work. Leaders should acknowledge the hard work of change by rewarding the early adopters, recognizing participants, and celebrating small wins, especially if a change will be lengthy (more than six months).

- *Concerns About Competence.* People resist change when they're worried that their skills will be obsolete. Leaders should provide abundant information, education, training, mentors, and support systems. Employees may be worried about their jobs, and whether they will have a job after the change occurs. Share what you can, especially if the change could impact employee's roles.

Leaders should avoid the temptation to craft changes in secret and then announce them all at once. It's better to plant seeds, sprinkle hints of what might be coming, and seek input. And it's important not to implement too many changes at one time. Overhauling entire departments and processes at once, can be distracting and confusing and cause productivity to plummet. Whenever possible keep things familiar and implement the changes incrementally.

Here is a simple example of a change management curve as illustrated in the change management model below. The dotted line represents when a well-thought-out change management process is designed. The solid line represents what occurs in most situations when a change management process is not well implemented.

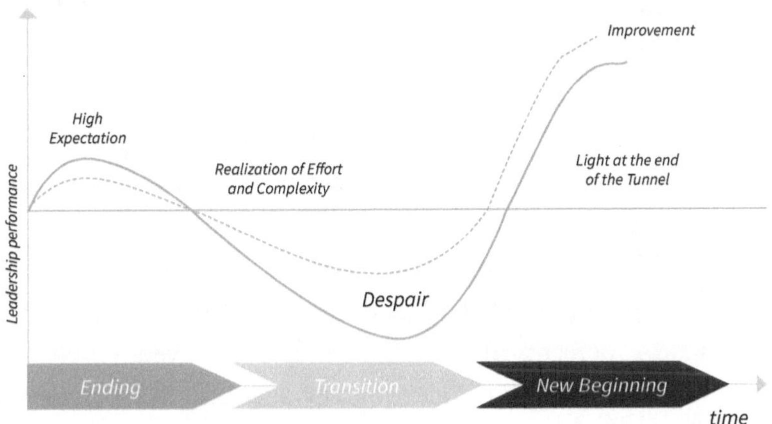

Why Change Management Is Essential

A well-developed change management strategy and implementation plan are essential to achieving success and sustainable organizational change as seen from the following statistics from the Gartner Group,[1] a leading global research and advisory firm providing actionable insights, tools, and consulting to business leaders across IT, finance, HR, and other sectors:

- Approximately 70 percent of change initiatives fail
- 28 percent of change initiatives are abandoned before completion
- 46 percent are behind schedule or over budget

Modern business environments are characterized by a relentless pace of transformation driven by many factors such as technological advancements, shifting consumer preferences, globalization, and unforeseen events like the COVID-19 pandemic. These changes can take various forms, and organizations must adapt to stay relevant and competitive.

- Only one-third of major change initiatives fully meet the goals set by the organization.[2]
- 50 percent of leaders don't know whether recent organizational changes have succeeded.[3]
- 74 percent of leaders say they involved employees in creating a change strategy, but only 42 percent of employees feel included.[4]

10 Step Process for Change

Vision & Commit

1. Create the specific vision and mission for your organization. It should answer the questions – Why are you making the change? and What will the company look like after the change? It must be compelling and inspiring.
2. Gain senior leadership commitment and sponsorship for the change.

Plan, Align & Mobilize

3. Develop a change program or process with senior leadership to include measures of success and behavioral changes that need to occur.
4. Review and change HR systems and processes as needed to facilitate the change as it occurs.
5. Develop rewards and recognition programs aligned with success measures and behavior change.

Design & Implement

6. Review and update job descriptions and/or roles to align with new competencies that are required to fill the new positions, succeed in those roles, and be promoted.
7. Ensure mid-level managers have requisite capability to do their jobs in the new environment. If

> they don't, how will they be trained to enable their success?
>
> 8. Implement the change program. What will be done to inspire, engage, and empower managers to change?
> 9. Create success measures to measure achievement. What's going well? Where is help needed? Then determine a roll out strategy for the rest of the organization.
> 10. Evaluate successes and areas of concern and adjust as necessary.

Where does change begin? Change needs to start with the CEO or owner and the executive team. They need to create a strong business case on why is the change is needed now, including what are the pros and the cons of the change from both a financial and productivity perspective. If there isn't a clear and compelling reason for the change, then it may not be the right time to make the change.

Having a change champion is also critical. This is the one person who is leading the change within the organization. It can't be the collective executive or leadership team. It needs to be one person who is 100 percent committed to drive the change forward.

Is the executive team prepared to go through the change curve? The executive team must be willing to walk the talk, meaning that they need to openly talk about the rationale for making the change and how they are feeling personally about going through the change themselves. It can't be overstated how important communication is during the change process. The more the better here. I'm many cases, I tell clients going through major change that you will get sick of talking about it, but you need to keep talking about it to your employees. Most major changes fail due to a lack of communication or setting unreasonable expectations on what the change will do for the company.

As the change is being implemented—whether it is a relatively simple change, such as implementing a new payroll system, or complex change, such as implementing a new enterprise resource planning system in a manufacturing company—it is essential to talk about why the change is occurring. The more challenging and complex the change the more important explaining the why.

Are mid-level managers kept in the loop? It is important to keep managers in the loop so when employees ask them questions, they know the answers and can champion the change. Many changes fail because the mid and first level managers are in the dark along with the employees. When a direct report asks them questions, if they don't know the answer, the opportunity to promote the vision is lost.

When making company-wide changes, you need to do a tremendous amount of planning up front and create a thorough communications and change management plan and process. If you plan for changes well, the chances for success will greatly increase. If you don't, you are setting yourself up to fail.

Chapter Thirteen

Professional Advisors

You may have heard that it takes a village to raise a child. The adage also applies to managing your human resource department. In this chapter, we'll explore the different strategic partners and relationships you may need to support and properly run the HR function at your company. The information is generic to be helpful to every company. Your specific needs may vary, depending on your company's current size and growth trajectory.

Companies with fewer than thirty employees may decide to work with a professional employer organization or PEO. A PEO is an outside company that can provide HR tactical services including payroll and onboarding, healthcare benefits, liability or property and casualty insurance, and some basic level of HR support for employee issues that arise. There are several very good ones out there. This could be a viable solution for smaller companies.

At some point, a PEO will no longer be a cost-effective solution for your company. PEO costs are driven by your number of employees. The more employees, the higher the cost of your PEO. Typically, once a company reaches about thirty employees, a PEO is no longer cost-effective.

When moving away from the PEO model, here is the basic line-up of the key partners you need to support your business:

- **Human Resources Information System (HRIS).** More than payroll processing HRIS's provide services such as virtual employee files storage, onboarding, applicant tracking, and performance management. The advantage for using an HRIS tool is that all the mandatory paperwork and employee forms associated with each employee are securely housed in a system that keeps confidential employee information truly confidential. The other advantage is you can find all your employee information in one place.

- **Healthcare Benefits Broker.** These brokers provide your employees with a variety of health care benefits coverage for themselves and their family.

- **Property and Casualty (P&C) Broker.** These brokers provide liability insurance for your company and its assets (including your building and possibly vehicles) and worker's compensation. In many cases benefits and P&C brokers may work for the same company. They are usually different people, though, because insurance needs are so vastly different.

- **Business Banker.** It is ideal to have a business account with a local banker who focuses on lower- and middle-market companies. In many cases, the banker may specialize in your industry vertical and know the market very well. Getting at least one good banking relationship established before the company is even formed is highly advisable. In many cases, having at least two business bankers from two different banks is advisable.

- **Business Attorney**. Ideally, you should have a good business attorney handle the basic business articles to form your company in the state in which you do business. If your business is a partnership or has multiple owners, you want to involve an attorney to draft the business agreements in case the partnership changes or dissolves or ownership changes in any way.
- **Employment Attorney.** In addition to your business attorney, you will need an employment attorney to counsel you on employment law. Often a mid-sized law firm will have business and employment attorneys on staff.
- **Certified Public Accountant (CPA).** You will need a CPA to help you with company financials and filing your company taxes and possibly your personal taxes, depending on the size of your business and how it's structured. As the company grows, your accounting needs will change, and your CPA firm needs may change also.
- **401K Broker.** These brokers provide a 401K retirement for your employees. You do not need to offer a 401K to employees when you start your company, but as your company grows, offering a 401K to help employees plan for their retirement could be an excellent idea. The company match usually vests over four to five years, so if the employee leaves the company in two years, they only get a percentage of the company contribution. The matching process can be a great employee retention tool.
- **Fractional Executives**. These are seasoned C-suite leaders (CFO, CMO, COO, CHRO) who provide

part-time, ongoing strategic guidance to companies on a short-term basis. They tend to be in specific firms in different disciplines, such as finance or accounting, information technology (IT), human resources (my firm's focus), and sales and marketing. The significant advantage of having contract experts is that you don't need to hire a full-time C-level executive to provide you with the critical expertise needed in areas of your business that are not its core functions. You get expertise on a fractional basis, which can be highly cost effective for your business in the short term or long term, depending on the growth plans for your business.

- **Business Coach.** A good business coach can help you create a good operating system or strategic planning process for your business. Many of these coaches have a formalized process. Other coaches may work exclusively with the business owner, CEO, or president as an outside confidante or trusted advisor to grow your business or even help you get your business prepared for a sales transaction in the future.

This overview is a sample of what most companies need to think through and the partners they need to have on their team to run a successful company. As mentioned, it does "take a village" to run and scale a successful business for long-term success.

Summary

As you read through the chapters, you may have identified with many of the scenarios here. My hope is that you will be able to use this book as an HR playbook in establishing your human resource processes, systems, and tools.

As your business grows, you may discover that the major issues slowing your growth are your people and the lack of a well-defined strategy or consistently documented and applied HR processes. You scale a business by creating processes for every function within the business, including HR. It's not rocket science; it's just good business.

You may be saying to yourself, "How does this guy know my company so well?" Most SMBs struggle with the same issues.

I find it extremely rewarding working with business owners and executives, PE firms, CEOs, and non-profit leaders to understand their pain points and solve their people issues. My company, HR Catalyst is composed of highly skilled HR leaders who create customized solutions to solve people issues for our clients. Each company is different; therefore, we do not offer cookie cutter solutions, but create a customized solution for your business.

A big differentiator for us is that we are not professional consultants. We are professional HR leaders who grew up in HR with many "best in class" companies in the Fortune 500 arena. We not only help you create a strategic people plan, but we are also very comfortable getting our hands dirty when needed. We partner with you to work through issues and minimize your risk as much as possible.

If your company has reached a point where you need to get help on the human resources or people side of your business, I would be thrilled to talk to you about the specific needs of your business, understand your pain points, and determine how HR Catalyst can help.

If you need a speaker for your business, professional group, or trade organization, I am available for engagements on all subjects involving human resources and how to build a successful people strategy in your business. I have spoken to many organizations and at national conferences.

At the end of the day, I'm a servant leader, who is blessed to do the work that I do and most importantly enjoy helping business or non-profit leaders solve their HR or people problems. If you get the people side of your business working effectively, this will translate into a more profitable and well-run business.

References

Books

The Five Dysfunctions of a Team by Patrick Lencioni
The Ideal Team Player by Patrick Lencioni
The Advantage by Patrick Lencioni
The Six Types of Working Genius by Patrick Lencioni
Servant Leadership by Norman Greenleaf
Start With Why by Simon Sinek
Leaders Eat Last by Simon Sinek
The Infinite Game by Simon Sinek
Good to Great by Jim Collins
Built to Last by Jim Collins & Jerry Porras
Drive by Daniel Pink
To Sell Is Human by Daniel Pink
Leading Change by John Kotter
Change by John Kotter
Leadership and Self-deception by The Arbinger Institute
Radical Candor by Kim Scott
Maximize Business Value by Tom Bronson
Maximize Business Value Playbook by Tom Bronson

Podcasts

At the Table by Patrick Lencioni
HR Problem Solver by Mark Mitford

Connect with the Author

For more information on HR Catalyst services go to www. hrcatalystconsulting.com

For a free consultation with the author, go to our website and use the Schedule a Call button that will link you to Mark Mitford's calendar

To hire Mark Mitford for speaking contact him at his email directly: mmitford@hrcatalystconsulting.com Mark is a dynamic speaker who has spoken to professional and non-profit groups of 20 to over 200 in his career on the importance of people in your business and how they can directly impact your financial performance.

Visit HR Catalyst's YouTube Channel for our podcasts, webinars and other videos

HR Catalyst's Podcast "HR Problem Solver" can be found on all major podcast listings

Connect with me on LinkedIn where I share relevant HR subject matter regularly

Notes

Chapter Two: Company Culture

1   Gallup, The Benefits of Employee Engagement, June 20, 2013, https://www.gallup.com/workplace/236927/employee-engagement-drives-growth.aspx.

2   Zach Blumenfeld, "I spent a day emerged in the Zappos Culture, here's what I learned," April 21, 2020, CultureCon, https://www.cultureconusa.org/post/zappos-company-culture-trip-what-i-learned#:~:text=Zappos'%20company%20culture%20is%20characterized%20by:%20*,organization%20that%20replaces%20the%20conventional%20management%20hierarchy.

Chapter Three: Recruiting

1   Samantha McLaren, "6 Stats That Will Change the Way You Write Job Posts," LinkedIn Talent Blog, January 24, 2019.

Chapter Four: Onboarding

1   https://www.shrm.org/topics-tools/topics/onboarding

2   Bruce Crumley, "Why Bad Onboarding Could Cost Your Business Nearly Half Your New Hires," Inc. magazine, September 2, 2025, https://www.inc.com/bruce-crumley/why-bad-onboarding-could-cost-your-business-nearly-half-your-new-hires/91234340.

3   Michael Moon, "Making the Business Case for Employee Learning Programs," Aberdeen Research, October 9, 2015, https://www.aberdeen.com/hcm-essentials/making-the-business-case-for-employee-learning-programs/.

Chapter Seven: Leadership Development

1   Kelsey Casselbury, "How to Measure the ROI of Leadership Development, SHRM, June 12, 2025, https://www.shrm.org/topics-tools/news/hr-magazine/how-to-measure-roi-leadership-development#:~:text=Calculating%20the%20return%20on%20investment%20(ROI)%20for,total%20program%20cost%20x%20100%20=%20ROI.

Chapter Ten: Employee Engagement

1   March 2020 was at the start of the COVID-19 pandemic, so that didn't factor into the original ratings.

Chapter Twelve: Change Management

1   Gartner Group: Change Management Risk: Understand the Causes and Consequences 16 July 2025- ID G00835218.

2   Kotter, J. P, *A Force of Change: How Leadership Differs from Management* (New York: Free Press, 1990).

3   Kotter, *A Force of Change.*

4   Gartner Group.